RONALD RE
IN GOD I T

RONALD REAGAN: IN GOD I TRUST

*Written and Compiled
by David R. Shepherd*

Tyndale House Publishers, Inc.
Wheaton, Illinois

First printing, August 1984

Library of Congress Catalog Card Number 84-51772
ISBN 0-8423-5704-1
Copyright 1984 by B.A.C. and Associates

CONTENTS

Acknowledgements

There are many people to thank who helped with the writing, compiling, and publishing of this book.

First, I should thank my wife, Cherie, and our church in Nashville for praying me through the tight production schedule. Herbert E. Ellingwood, Edwin Meese, Ben Elliot, Faith Whittlesey, Doug Holladay, and Elliot Abrams were most gracious to agree to interviews on short notice and to provide valuable background information.

Thank you's go to my research assistant, David Ayers, for mining much of the raw material and to my secretary, Felicity Carr, for her diligence in processing all these words.

My business associate, Woody Wojdylak, is to be thanked for seeing the need for this book to be published. Mark Taylor, Dr. Wendell Hawley, Bill Noller, Ken Petersen, and others at Tyndale House have my sincere gratitude for granting me this opportunity and for their total commitment to the publishing of this book.

Last but certainly not least, I thank President Reagan for being so quotable and, most of all, for being a leader who trusts in the Lord.

David R. Shepherd
Nashville, Tennessee
July 1984

ONE

WHATEVER DAYS ARE LEFT

March 30, 1981, was a dull, gray rainy day in Washington, D.C. It was also Ronald Reagan's seventieth day as America's fortieth president.

There was nothing unusual about the president's schedule on this particular Monday. He was up early to attend a breakfast with 140 sub-Cabinet-level officers in the East Room. Afterward, he attended a meeting with his senior staff in the Oval Office and then was briefed by national security advisors. Later in the morning, he greeted Hispanic leaders and discussed his efforts to place Hispanics in government positions.

He had lunch in the family quarters of the White House, worked on a speech he would give in the afternoon, and then stretched out for a brief rest.

At 1:45 P.M. the president climbed into his limousine for a seven-minute ride to the Washington Hilton where he would address 3,500 labor union representatives, the largest group to hear him speak since Inauguration Day. During his eighteen-minute speech, one sentence seemed prophetic. "Violent crime has surged 10 percent, making neighborhood streets unsafe and families fearful in their homes," he said.

As President Reagan left the hotel to return to the White House, his typical workday suddenly became historic. While pausing by his limousine to wave to reporters and other onlookers, Ronald Reagan became the fifth American president to be struck by a bullet.

To those who vividly remember the assassination of a president, a presidential candidate, and a civil rights leader, the news of John Hinckley, Jr.'s, assassination attempt seemed like a bad dream. What made matters worse were the incomplete reports that came via the news media. One minute the nation was relieved that the president was unharmed in the attack. The next minute he was in surgery for the removal of a bullet close to his heart. Then there was the added trauma of the three other men who were wounded during the attack.

Six shots fired in two seconds struck four men and made history. But Americans were spared the ultimate national nightmare of burying a slain leader, because Ronald Reagan was the first American president to be struck by a bullet and live.

During the days that followed, the nation observed President Reagan's recovery process. Most memorable were the reports of his bravery and good humor, which endeared him in the hearts of the American people and set national tensions at ease.

He amazed everyone. Soon after the shooting, just before surgery, the president remarked to Mrs. Reagan, "Honey, I forgot to duck." And as he entered the operating room, he joked with doctors, saying, "Please tell me that you're all Republicans." Then, after surgery, he had the presence of mind to deliver this one-liner: "All in all, I'd rather be in Philadelphia."

The day after the shooting, the president and Mrs. Reagan were visited by the now late Cardinal Terence Cooke. It was during this visit that the president delivered his most profound and least publicized one-liner of the entire ordeal. After discussing the experience with the cardinal, the president said, "Whatever days are left to me are his."

These words, which he later repeated publically during the 1982 National Prayer Breakfast, are perhaps the most important words of his presidency to date. They are the benchmark by which the value of his administration can be measured and judged. For it is in these words that the power of the Reagan presidency is revealed.

Ronald Reagan's words and actions as president reveal a moral framework, a fixed set of values based on Judeo-Christian principles found in the Bible. It appears, from what he has said, that he has settled in his own mind many of life's basic questions and has brought to the presidency a distinctively Judeo-Christian world view of history and current events.

His public statements suggest that he was motivated to seek political office, first as California's governor and then as president, because of his philosophy of life, not as the result of some vocational preference. His commitment to this biblical philosophy, which openly recognizes God as his source of values, is clear.

The attack on his life seems only to have deepened his faith in God and strengthened his commitment to those spiritual values. Perhaps as he thought about his scrape with death, he realized that his life had been spared and that God had a profound purpose for the remainder of his days. To commit the rest of his life to the Lord in this way was a natural response for a man who already had felt a calling upon his life to be president.

Proverbs 21:1 says, "The king's heart is in the hand of the Lord; he directs it like a watercourse wherever he pleases." How pleased the Lord must be with a leader who does not resist that turning.

"Well, then, if the president is so religious why doesn't

he go to church?" This has become a favorite question of late among those who take a dim view of "mixing religion with politics."

The news media have also picked up the question ("Who's a 'Good Christian'?" *Newsweek,* August 6, 1984), making the president's Christian faith an issue. During a March 1984 question-and-answer session with news reporters, the president was asked, "Are you going to church this Sunday, sir? The Democrats say you talk about religion but you don't go to church."

The president responded, "Yes, I've noticed that. . . . I haven't bothered to check on their attendance, but I think they must be aware of why I have not been attending. . . . I represent too much of a threat to too many other people for me to be able to go to church. And frankly, I miss it very much."

The Reverend Donn D. Moomaw, pastor of the Bel Air Presbyterian Church in Los Angeles, has come to the President's defense in this matter of church attendance.

Moomaw says that the Reagans regularly attended his church, beginning in 1963. Even while Mr. Reagan was governor, he and his family attended the church whenever they were at their home in Los Angeles. More often than not, they would drive their own car, visit with other worshipers, and leave with little inconvenience to anyone.

However, when Mr. Reagan became an announced candidate for the presidency, all of that changed. For security reasons, federal, state, and local law enforcement officers began accompanying him to church. More than twenty Secret Service cars, twenty-five motorcycle policemen, ten to twelve SWAT squads, and scores of press people swarmed over the church premises. Secret Service men and women stood silently at all the doors, checking people as they entered the church building. SWAT squad members stood guard on the roof with their rifles in hand while helicopters soared overhead.

The Reagans, of course, were given very little choice in the matter of security measures.

Since the attempt on the president's life, and because of the daily threats of violence to him and his wife, he has chosen to take the advice of many, including Billy Graham, and limit his attendance at church. The Reagans do not wish to subject any congregation to the distractions created by necessary security precautions.

Moomaw says that the Reagans have chosen not to have regular Sunday services in the White House for a variety of practical and personal reasons. Primarily they feel that church services in the White House would be self-serving, predictable, and religiously safe. They desire to worship with the body of Christ and be challenged by the full responsibility of Christian discipleship.

According to Moomaw, president and Mrs. Reagan are committed Christians; prayer and Bible reading are an indispensable part of their lives. He believes they have made the wisest decision by choosing to worship God in alternative ways at this time in their lives.

Despite this testimony from both the president and his pastor, there are many who believe that the president's "religious talk" is merely an attempt to get more votes.

Some live by the adage, "Never trust a cross-eyed preacher or a praying politician." It's difficult if not impossible for them to understand that President Reagan or anyone in political office can be vocal about faith in Christ and promote traditional moral values without having an ulterior motive.

Others simply do not know the facts about the president's Christian upbringing or about his personal decision to accept Christ as his Lord and Savior. Despite his years of public service, they are surprised to discover his deep faith and trust in God.

Whatever the reason, President Reagan's spiritual heart remains a mystery to the public, the media, and his associates alike. But this isn't unusual for someone in Ronald Reagan's position.

The Book of Proverbs, written by a king, says, "As the heavens are high and the earth is deep, so the hearts of kings are unsearchable." In other words, leaders of nations are sometimes hard to figure out.

Ronald Reagan is no different. He is a ruler—a leader of a nation and the free world—and his heart is unsearchable. However, there is another truth in Scripture which applies to him. Jesus said that out of the abundance of the heart, the mouth speaks. That is to say, the heart is the reservoir of man's true thoughts and the mouth is the outlet for them.

During the past four years, the president has given us insights into the thoughts of his spiritual heart. In numerous speeches and interviews, he has spoken often regarding matters of faith in God, traditional values, prayer, the Bible, family, the sanctity of life, and America's spiritual heritage.

The purpose of this book is to let the president speak for himself. This has been done by compiling many of his public statements about moral issues and matters of personal faith. For those desiring to better understand the spiritual aspect of the president's personal life, these statements offer intriguing glimpses of Ronald Reagan the man, the leader, and the Christian.

T W O

A FAITH REVEALED

On January 30, 1984, President Reagan addressed the annual convention of the National Association of Religious Broadcasters. The speech was a good one. The president articulated many of the themes he had spoken on so many times before—faith, the importance of spiritual values, prayer, the Bible, and the family. The president felt at home with the group, and he was enthusiastically received.

However, the president's remarks, which on the surface may have seemed routine, given the audience, struck quite a different chord with the news media. It seems that for the first time the media made the discovery that Ronald Reagan unabashedly has a specific and definite faith in Jesus Christ.

The New York Times reacted strongly to the president's statements of faith in Christ. In a February 3, 1984, editorial titled "Sermon on the Stump," editors of the *Times* criticized the president for "pandering to the Christian right that helped to propel his national political career." They said, "Americans ask piety in Presidents, not displays of religious preference."

Two weeks after the speech, President Reagan was interviewed by members of the Knight-Ridder News Service. The NRB speech was brought up by a reporter and discussed by the President. What follows are portions of that question and answer session:

Reporter: Mr. President, I'd like to ask you . . . a question about something that may be a little delicate, but it's nevertheless been on my mind and on the minds of several people.

I was at your speech to the National Association of Religious Broadcasters, and as others have commented, you've never been much to wear religion on your sleeve one way or the other. But I wonder if . . . preaching the gospel of Christ . . . isn't a bit divisive and whether it might not be wise, especially since there are a heck of a lot of people in this country who are not of the same persuasion. It just doesn't seem like you in the past, and that's why I'm asking.

The President: Maybe others haven't listened to me in the past. I remember once, long before I was even the Governor of California, when I was just out of the mashed-potato circuit, I was invited to speak to a national meeting of military chaplains. They'd been having a three-day meeting in California. And afterward, one of them came up to me . . . , shook my hand, and said that I was the first person in their three-day meeting who had mentioned the name of Christ.

No, it isn't easy for me to talk about this . . . but I do believe that there is, and has been . . . a great hunger for a kind of spiritual revival in this country, for people to believe again in things that they once believed in—basic truths and all. Obviously, speaking to religious broadcasters, I would speak more on that subject than I would, say, to the Chamber of Commerce. . . .

The fall of any empire, any great civilization, has been preceded by it forsaking its gods. . . . I don't want us to be another great civilization that began its decline by forsaking its God. . . .

I also feel that there is a responsibility in this position—as Teddy Roosevelt called it, "a bully pulpit"—to do those things. I was criticized for speaking about school prayer in the House Chamber at the State of the Union address. But am I not correct that above my head, engraved in the wall . . . was "one nation under God"?

Reporter: I'm speaking of a specific kind of religion. The allusions to the Christian gospel and to Christ as coming from a president who is a man in a nonsectarian office.

The President: Yes. But . . . at the lighting of the Christmas tree . . . I said that on that birthday [of] the man from Galilee, . . . there are those in our land who recognized him as a prophet or a great teacher . . . and there are those of us who believe that he was of divine origin and the Son of God. And, whichever, we celebrated his birthday with respect for the man.

This exchange is enlightening for a number of reasons, but it primarily illustrates a seeming paradox which exists in the life of the president with regard to his Christian faith. On one hand, he considers his personal faith in Christ a private matter and does not put it on public display. On the other hand, he is very open and comfortable with discussing and applying principles of his faith when it comes to his job.

Presidential Counselor Edwin Meese, who is also a close personal friend of the president's, talks about these two sides of the president.

"The president feels a person's religious beliefs are a

very private matter," Meese explains. "He has never tried to exploit them or utilize them for political purposes.

"At the same time, he feels a Christian has an obligation, when the opportunity comes up naturally, not to be reticent about professing his faith. Of all the people I've ever known, I have never known anyone less uncomfortable about discussing religious matters in a very matter-of-fact and confident way. To him, this is an important part of his life, and when the subject comes up, he is not at all hesitant to talk about it—and this was true way back in California."

A close look at the president's public statements supports the truth of Meese's assessment. Few if any official public remarks can be found in which the president draws attention to details of his personal faith in Christ. He makes no public claims to be a certain kind of Christian and makes no promises to the nation that in any way would exploit God or God's Word for his personal gain. His piety remains personal, and details of it are only revealed when he is questioned about it or when close associates discuss it with others.

For example, it is known that President Reagan is a born again Christian because another close friend of his, Herbert E. Ellingwood, has talked privately with him about it and chose to publish this fact in an article in the November 1980 issue of *Christian Life* magazine.

In that same article, Ellingwood, who served as chairman for the 1983 Year of the Bible observance, also reveals other information about the president that more than likely will not appear in many presidential speeches:

1. Ronald Reagan has a good understanding of the Bible because his deeply religious mother took him to Sunday school regularly. He has also been a Sunday school teacher.

2. His favorite Bible verse is John 3:16. When asked

what it means to him personally, he responds, "It means that having accepted Jesus Christ as my Savior, I have God's promise of eternal life in heaven, as well as the abundant life here on earth that he promises to each of us in John 10:10."

3. He has responded to questions from Christian leaders and shared his faith with such people as Billy Graham, Demos Shakarian, Bob Mumford, the board of *New Wine* magazine, and Pope Paul VI.

In Frank Van der Linden's book, *The Real Reagan* (Morrow), still more is revealed about the president's personal spiritual life through private discussions that he had with Christian leaders.

Mr. Van der Linden reports that candidate Reagan met with George Otis of High Adventure Ministries in 1976 and with the Reverend Adrian Rogers, then president of the Southern Baptist Convention in 1980. Here is an excerpt from those conversations:

> *Otis*: Have you been born again?
>
> *Reagan*: Yes. I can't remember a time in my life when I didn't call upon God and hopefully thank him as often as I called upon him.
>
> *Otis*: Do you really believe somebody is listening up there?
>
> *Reagan*: Oh, my! If I didn't believe that, I'd be scared to death!

Rogers, who met with Reagan early in the primary campaign of 1980, cross-examined the governor at length. Rogers said afterward: "Governor Reagan said that his faith is very personal, that God is real to him. He had a personal experience when he invited Christ into his life. I asked if he knew the Lord Jesus or just knew 'about' him. Reagan replied: 'I *know* him.' "

The Real Reagan also gives us other insights into the spiritual upbringing and character of the president:

1. He was raised in the Disciples of Christ church and attended Eureka College, a school maintained by this denomination.

2. He has never consulted a psychiatrist. He is very secure mentally, emotionally, and psychologically, which is a direct result of his Christian faith.

3. He is remarkably calm and peaceful, which comes directly from his belief that God has a divine plan and purpose for his life.

4. He entered the 1976 presidential race only after much meditation and prayer.

5. Before moving to Washington, the Reagan family attended worship services at the Bel Air Presbyterian Church and often sought spiritual guidance from its pastor, the Reverend Donn Moomaw. Moomaw told an interviewer that he and Reagan "have spent many hours together on their knees."

As interesting as these personal glimpses are, the point is that they usually come through others close to him or from the president only when he is specifically asked to comment on his personal faith. He is very careful to avoid making his piety an issue. For example, during elections, he does not campaign in churches. He chooses to address any Christian constituency from a public forum and discuss political and social issues that are of concern to them.

However, when it comes to Ronald Reagan's vision for America and what it takes to make and keep America great, he is not the least bit shy about stating his deeply held convictions that are based solely on his faith in God and his moral world view.

He feels his faith in this instance should not be limited to private conversations and interviews, because he is a firm believer in Benjamin Franklin's statement: "He who introduces into public office the principles of primitive Christianity will change the face of the world."

Ronald Reagan goes public with principles of his Christian faith because he believes that he was destined to have a part in shaping the nation's destiny. Some have called it his compulsion to make America great again. He would say that he has felt called to lead the nation.

This inner drive is reflected in a statement that he made repeatedly from the time he left the governorship to the time he was elected president: "The time has come to turn back to God and reassert our trust in him for the healing of the nation."

Those who say that the president has suddenly become religious in order to take advantage of the support of the "Religious Right" are misinformed and have failed to see or understand the dynamic of his leadership. The president's vision for the nation predates the establishment of the Moral Majority and the recent phenomenon of Christian political action. In no way can it be construed that Ronald Reagan tested the political winds in order to pander after the Christian vote. Even if he had wanted to, there were no political winds blowing that direction back in the 1960s, when he was beginning to speak more openly about his vision for America.

Many Christians at that time were still living with the mistaken notion that believers should not be involved in anything so blatantly secular as politics. They were ignorantly content to let humanistic philosophies get stronger footholds in our system of government, resulting in laws that we are finding difficult to live with today. If there were many Christians at that time who believed otherwise, they found a home in the great "Silent Majority" of the 1970s.

The truth is that the Christian political activists of today found Ronald Reagan and followed him. If anything, Reagan could have said, "Hey, what took you all so long?"

Mr. Ellingwood relates an early encounter with Governor Reagan just after he was first elected:

> Inauguration week in January 1967 provided some cautious optimism to Christians. This new governor, Ronald Reagan, at a prayer breakfast stated: "Belief in the dependence on God is essential to our state and nation. This will be an integral part of our state as long as I have anything to do with it."
> Was that rhetoric? A politician's prayer? It was the beginning of the Jesus movement for young people on southern California beaches and in the canyons. But no one had heard "Jesus words" in the campaign.

The Governor's Prayer Breakfast in 1972 gave Reagan another opportunity to share his belief that God does have and can provide an answer to social problems: "I think our nation and the world need a spiritual revival as it has never been needed before . . . a simple answer . . . a profound and complete solution to all the trouble we face."

While introducing Billy Graham to a rally in southern California, Reagan stated, "There is no need in our land today greater than the need to rediscover our spiritual heritage. Why is a representative of government here? To welcome with humble pride a man whose mission in life has been to remind us that in all our seeking, in all our confusion, the answer to each problem is to be found in the simple words of Jesus of Nazareth, who urged us to love one another."

Reagan's view of government's role in his vision for America is also nothing new. Consider this excerpt from an early speech by the governor: "I believe this nation hungers for a spiritual revival; hungers to once again see honor placed above political expediency; to see government once again the protector of our liberties, not the distributor of

gifts and privilege. Government should uphold, not under-
mine those institutions which are custodians of the very
values upon which civilization is founded—religion, education, and above all, family."

Enough? There is lots more where that came from.
These have been consistent themes for the better part of
the president's adult life. He is unwavering in these convictions and they undergird every decision he makes, whether
it be in economic policy, foreign affairs, or social issues.

As long as Reagan is allowed to be Reagan, it will
always be so.

THREE

THE ABUNDANCE OF HIS HEART

While campaigning for the presidency in 1980, Ronald Reagan continued to share the same message he had been preaching since the 1960s. For the first time in his career as a public servant, he truly had a national platform from which he could communicate his vision for America. Also for the first time, all Americans had the opportunity to hear, examine, and pass judgment on the major tenants of his plan for the nation's future.

Something he said must have rung true with the majority of voters in 1980, because candidate Reagan became President Reagan in one of the greatest landslide election victories in American history.

Because of his communication skills and persuasive manner, he has been nicknamed "The Great Communicator." Administration officials admit that if a certain policy is to succeed, the president must be involved in making the case for it both with Congress and the American people.

While the president's gift for communicating has been a tremendous asset to him, the real reason for his success is his sincerity. He actually believes all those things he says! To say that his words are just political rhetoric, one either does not know him very well or believes that former actors are not capable of being honest.

Suspicion of the president's sincerity is especially acute with regard to his spiritual statements. Aides say that one of the charges they hear most often is that he is using religion for political purposes—in others words, demagoguery. A common question, even among Christians, is, "Are those really his words, or does he just say what his speechwriters tell him to say?" It seems that for some believers, it is almost too good to be true that a president in these modern times would be such an advocate of Judeo-Christian principles. (Many nonbelievers wish it were not so true.)

A look at the speechwriting process as conducted by president Reagan reveals that he is very much in charge of the words he speaks and most certainly takes responsibility for those words.

The president has had years of experience not only in speechmaking, but also in speechwriting. He enjoys writing his own speeches and is good at it. In the early days of his presidency, he wrote many of his own remarks. However, with the ever-increasing demands on his time, he has had to depend more on writers to help him organize his speeches. The president, though, is still very active in the research and writing of his messages. Before an address, the writers spend time with him in order to hear him articulate major points he wants covered in the address. They also receive from him specific information that needs to be included.

Ben Elliot, chief speechwriter at the White House, says the president often sends him information that he has come across in his personal reading or will forward quotes from men and women that he thinks are particularly interesting or inspiring. These are included in the president's messages where they are appropriate.

After putting together a draft of the speech, the president carefully reviews it and makes all the necessary changes.

Often he rewrites complete sections or adds new information.

The president is just as concerned about remarks that are written for small groups as he is about major addresses such as the State of the Union. Faith Whittlesey, special assistant to the president for Public Liasion, has often seen the president take prepared remarks for constituency groups and discard them completely in favor of his own handwritten note cards. "We work hard many times in this office to put together what we think he should say to certain groups," Mrs. Whittlesey explains. "And then we get into the meeting and nowhere do we see our little piece of paper. He has his own remarks written out in hand, with his black pen, underlined—all handwritten—that he has done the night before the meeting."

One specific example Mrs. Whittlesey recalls was a speech the president made to a large group of Christian fundamentalists. "We struggled with that speech and went back and forth with the speechwriters about exactly what would be submitted to the president," she says. "Well, he completely discarded the speech we recommended and took his own remarks to the meeting. After all of our work, he chose to talk about a report written by a Jewish chaplain stationed in Lebanon. That's what moved him."

Why is the president so careful about the words he speaks? Because he cannot talk about anything that does not truly come from his heart. To do so would violate his integrity.

Mr. Van der Linden in *The Real Reagan* makes this observation: "He is . . . a philosopher and a moralist with firm convictions that he refused to compromise throughout his long quest for the presidency. He knows who he is; he knows precisely what he believes; he knows where he wants to take this country.

"Well aware that he may have only a few years left on this earth, the president moves through the autumn of his life with calm confidence that he conveys to a nation shaken by change and by fear of the future. Americans who look for a Big Daddy in the White House will not find one there. They will see, instead, a simple, earnest, courageous man who is seeking guidance from God."

FOUR

KEEPING THE FAITH

The President's Statements on Faith in God and the Importance of Spiritual Values

I have fought long and hard for my Lord, and through it all I have kept true to him (II Timothy 4:7, TLB).

National Prayer Breakfast
February 5, 1981

[An] unknown author wrote of a dream and in the dream was walking down the beach beside the Lord. As they walked, above him in the sky was reflected each stage and experience of his life. Reaching the end of the beach, and of his life, he turned back, looked down the beach, and saw the two sets of footprints in the sand. [But] he looked again and realized that every once in a while there was only one set of footprints. And each time there was only one set of footprints, it was when the experience reflected in the sky was one of despair, of desolation, of great trial or grief in his life.

[So] he turned to the Lord and said, "You said that if I would walk with you, you would always be beside me and take my hand. Why did you desert me? Why are you not there in my times of greatest need?" And the Lord said, "My child, I did not leave you. Where you see only one set of footprints, it was there that I carried you."

Abraham Lincoln once said, "I would be the most foolish person on this footstool earth if I believed for one moment that I could perform the duties assigned to me without the help of one who is wiser than all." I know that in the days to come and the years ahead there are going to be many times when there will only be one set of footprints in my life. If I did not believe that, I could not face the days ahead.

University of Notre Dame Commencement Exercise
May 17, 1981

For the West, for America, the time has come to dare to show to the world that our civilized ideas, our traditions, our values, are not—like the ideology and war machine of totalitarian societies—just a facade of strength. It is time for the world to know our intellectual and spiritual values are rooted in the source of all strength, a belief in a Supreme Being, and law higher than our own.

International Association of the Chiefs of Police Meeting
September 28, 1981

For all our science and sophistication, for all of our justified pride in intellectual accomplishment, we must never forget the jungle is always there waiting to take us over. Only our deep moral values and our strong social institutions can hold back that jungle and restrain the darker impulses of human nature.

New York City Partnership
January 14, 1982

The most powerful force in the world comes not from balance sheets or weapons arsenals, but from the human spirit. It flows like a mighty river in the faith, love, and determination that we share in our common ideals and aspirations.

National Prayer Breakfast Luncheon
February 4, 1982

Well, God is with us. We need only to believe. The psalmist says, "Weeping may endure for a night, but joy cometh in the morning."

Speaking for Nancy and myself, we thank you for all your prayers on our behalf. And it is true that you can sense and feel that power.

I've always believed that we were, each of us, put here for a reason, that there is a plan, somehow a divine plan for all of us. I know now that whatever days are left to me belong to him.

We have God's promise that what we give will be given back many times over, so let us go forth from here and rekindle the fire of our faith. Let our wisdom be vindicated by our deeds.

We are told in II Timothy that when our work is done, we can say, "We have fought the good fight. We have finished the race. We have kept the faith." This is an evidence of it.

National Religious Broadcasters Convention
February 9, 1982

The Book of St. John tells us, "For God so loved the world that he gave his only begotten Son that whosoever believeth in him should not perish but have everlasting life." We have God's promise that what we give will be given back many times over. And we also have his promise that we could take to heart with regard to our country—"That if my people who are called by my name humble themselves and pray and seek my face and turn from their wicked ways, then will I hear from heaven and will forgive their sins and heal their land."

Chamber of Commerce of the United States
April 26, 1982

The most powerful force for progress in this world doesn't come from government entities, public programs, or even precious resources like oil or gold. True wealth comes from the heart, from the treasure of ideas and spirit, from the investments of millions of brave people with hope for the future, trust in their fellow men, and faith in God.

Alfred M. Landon Lecture
September 9, 1982

I think the American people are hungry for a spiritual revival. More and more of us are beginning to sense that we can't have it both ways. We can't expect God to protect us in a crisis and just leave him over there on the shelf in our day-to-day living. I wonder if sometimes he isn't waiting for us to wake up. [I wonder if] he isn't maybe running out of patience.

Meeting with Editors and Publishers of Trade Magazines
September 24, 1982

I believe this country is hungry for a spiritual revival. I also believe that what Teddy Roosevelt said once is true—"The presidency is a bully pulpit." And we're not going to give up on those social issues that have to do with the morals of this country and the great standards that made this country great. We'll be working for them too.

National Religious Broadcasters Convention
January 31, 1983

All of us, as Protestants, Catholics, and Jews, have a special responsibility to remember our fellow believers who are being persecuted in other lands. We're all children of Abraham. We're children of the same God. . . .

This year, for the first time in history, the Voice of America broadcast a religious service worldwide—Christmas Eve at the National Presbyterian Church in Washington, D.C.

Now, these broadcasts are not popular with governments of totalitarian powers. But make no mistake, we have a duty to broadcast. Aleksandr Herzen, the Russian writer, warned, "To shrink from saying a word in defense of the oppressed is as bad as any crime." Well, I pledge to you that America will stand up, speak out, and defend the values we share. To those who would crush religious freedom, our message is plain: You may jail your believers. You may close their churches, confiscate their Bibles, and harass their rabbis and priests, but you will never destroy the love of God and freedom that burns in their hearts. They will triumph over you.

Malcolm Muggeridge, the brilliant English commentator, has written, "The most important happening in the world today is the resurgence of Christianity in the Soviet Union, demonstrating that the whole effort sustained over sixty years to brainwash the Russian people into accepting materialism has been a fiasco."

Think of it: the most awesome military machine in history, but it is no match for that one, single man, [a] hero, [the] strong yet tender, Prince of Peace. His name alone, Jesus, can lift our hearts, soothe our sorrows, heal our wounds, and drive away our fears. . . .

With his message and with your conviction and commitment, we can still move mountains. . . .

Before I say good-bye, I wanted to leave with you these words from an old Netherlands folk song, because they made me think of our meeting here today:

> We gather together to ask the Lord's
> blessing;
> We all do extol Thee, Thou Leader trium-
> phant,
> And pray that Thou still our Defender
> wilt be.
> Let Thy congregation escape tribulation:
> Thy name be ever praised! O Lord, make
> us free!

To which I would only add a line from another song: "America, America, God shed His grace on thee."

National Association of Evangelicals Convention
March 8, 1983

An evangelical minister and a politician arrived at heaven's gate one day together. St. Peter, after doing all the necessary formalities, took them in hand to show them where their quarters would be. And he took them to a small, single room with a bed, a chair, and a table and said this was for the clergyman. Well, the politician was a little worried about what might be in store for him. And he couldn't believe it when St. Peter stopped in front of a beautiful mansion with lovely grounds, many servants, and told him that these would be his quarters.

[So] he couldn't help but ask, "But wait, now—there's something wrong—how do I get this mansion while that good and holy man only gets a single room?" And St. Peter said, "You have to understand how things are up here. We've got thousands and thousands of clergy. You're the first politician who ever made it."

I don't want to contribute to a stereotype. So, I tell you there are a great many God-fearing, dedicated, noble men and women in public life. . . . And, yes, your help [is needed] to keep us ever mindful of the ideas and the principles that brought us into the public arena in the first place. The basis of those ideals and principles is a commitment to freedom and personal liberty that itself is grounded in the much deeper realization that freedom prospers only where the blessings of God are avidly sought and humbly accepted. . . .

I want you to know that this administration is motivated by a political philosophy that sees the greatness of America in you, her people, and in your families, churches, neighborhoods, communities—the institutions that foster and nourish values [such as] concern for others and respect for the rule of law under God.

Now, I don't have to tell you that this puts us in opposition to, or at least out of step with, a prevailing attitude of many who have turned to a modern-day secularism, discarding the tried and time-tested values upon which our very civilization is based. No matter how well intentioned, their value system is radically different from that of most Americans. And while they proclaim that they're freeing us from superstitions of the past, they've taken upon themselves the job of superintending us by government rule and regulation. Sometimes their voices are louder than ours, but they are not yet a majority.

An example of that vocal superiority is evident in a controversy now going on in Washington. And since I'm involved, I've been waiting to hear from the parents of young America. How far are they willing to go in giving to government their prerogatives as parents?

Let me state the case as briefly and simply as I can. An organization of citizens, sincerely motivated and deeply concerned about the increase in illegitimate births and abortions involving girls well below the age of consent, some time ago established a nationwide network of clinics to offer help to these girls and, hopefully, alleviate this situation. Now, again, let me say, I do not fault their intent. However, in their well-intentioned effort, these clinics have decided to provide advice and birth control drugs and devices to underage girls without the knowledge of their parents.

For some years now, the federal government has helped with funds to subsidize these clinics. In providing for this, the Congress decreed that every effort would be made to maximize parental participation. Nevertheless, the drugs and devices are prescribed without getting parental consent or giving notification after they've done so. Girls termed "sexually active"—and that has replaced the word "promiscuous"—are given this help in order to prevent illegitimate birth or abortion.

Well, we have ordered clinics receiving federal funds

to notify the parents such help has been given. One of the nation's leading newspapers has created the term "squeal rule" in editorializing against us for doing this, and we're being criticized for violating the privacy of young people. A judge has recently granted an injunction against an enforcement of our rule. I've watched TV panel shows discuss this issue, seen columnists' pontification on our error, but no one seems to mention morality as playing a part in the subject of sex.

Is all of Judeo-Christian tradition wrong? Are we to believe that something so sacred can be looked upon as a purely physical thing with no potential for emotional and psychological harm? And isn't it the parents' right to give counsel and advice to keep their children from making mistakes. that may affect their entire lives?

Many of us in government would like to know what parents think about this intrusion into their families by government. We're going to fight in the courts. The right of parents and the rights of family take precedence over those of Washington-based bureaucrats and social engineers.

But the fight against parental notification is really only one example of many attempts to water down traditional values and even abrogate the original terms of American democracy.

There's a great spiritual awakening in America, a renewal of the traditional values that have been the bedrock of America's goodness and greatness.

One recent survey by a Washington-based research council concluded that Americans were far more religious than the people of other nations. Ninety-five percent of those surveyed expressed a belief in God. A huge majority believed the Ten Commandments had real meaning in their lives. Another study has found that an overwhelming majority of Americans disapprove of adultery, teenage sex, pornography, abortion, and hard drugs. And this same study showed a deep reverence for the importance of family ties and religious belief.

There is sin and evil in the world, and we're enjoined by Scripture and the Lord Jesus to oppose it with all our might. . . .

Radio Address to the Nation
April 2, 1983

This week as American families draw together in worship, we join with millions upon millions of others around the world also celebrating the traditions of their faiths. . . .

This week Jewish families and friends have been celebrating Passover, a tradition rich in symbolism and meaning. Its observance reminds all of us that the struggle for freedom and the battle against oppression waged by Jews since ancient times is one shared by people everywhere. And Christians have been commemorating the last momentous days leading to the crucifixion of Jesus 1,950 years ago. Tomorrow, as morning spreads around the planet, we'll celebrate the triumph of life over death, the resurrection of Jesus. Both observances tell of sacrifice and pain but also of hope and triumph.

As we look around us today, we still find human pain and suffering, but we also see it answered with individual courage and spirit, strengthened by faith. For example, the brave Polish people, despite the oppression of a godless tyranny, still cling to their faith and their belief in freedom. Shortly after Palm Sunday mass this week, Lech Walesa faced a cheering crowd of workers outside a Gdansk church. He held his hand up in a sign of victory and predicted, "The time will come when we will win."

Recently, an East German professor, his wife, and two daughters climbed into a seven-foot rowboat and crossed the freezing, wind-whipped Baltic to escape from tyranny. Arriving in West Germany after a harrowing seven-hour, thirty-one-mile journey past East German border patrols, the man said he and his family had risked everything so that the children would have the chance to grow up in freedom.

In Central America, Communist-inspired revolution still spreads terror and instability, but it's no match for the much greater force of faith that runs so deep among the people. We saw this during Pope John Paul II's recent visit there. As he conducted a mass in Nicaragua, state police jeered and led organized heckling by Sandinista supporters. But the Pope lifted a crucifix above his head and waved it at the crowd before him, then turned and symbolically held it up before the massive painting of Sandinista soldiers that loomed behind. The symbol of good prevailed. In contrast, everywhere else the Holy Father went in the region, spreading a message that only love can build, he was met by throngs of enthusiastic believers, eager for papal guidance and blessing. . . .

While the San Diego-based U.S.S. Hoel steamed toward Melbourne, Australia, on Ash Wednesday, its crew heard of terrible brushfires sweeping two Australian states. More than seventy people were killed and the destruction was great. Well, the crew of this American ship raised $4,000 from their pockets to help, but they felt that it wasn't enough. So, leaving only a skeleton crew aboard, the one hundred American sailors gave up a day's shore leave, rolled up their sleeves, and set to work rebuilding a ruined community on the opposite end of the earth. Just Americans being Americans, but something for all of us to be proud of.

Stories like these—of men and women around the world who love God and freedom—bear a message of world hope and brotherhood like the rites of Passover and Easter that we celebrate this weekend.

A grade school class in Somerville, Massachusetts, recently wrote me to say, "We studied about countries and found out that each country in our world is beautiful and that we need each other. People may look a little different, but we're still people who need the same things." They said, "We want peace. We want to take care of one another. We want to be able to get along with one another. We want to be able to share. We want freedom and justice. We want to be friends. We want no wars. We want to be able to talk to one another. We want to be able to travel around the world without fear."

And then they asked, "Do you think that we can have these things one day?"

Well, I do. I really do. Nearly 2,000 years after the coming of the Prince of Peace, such simple wishes may still seem far from fulfillment. But we can achieve them. We must never stop trying.

Ceremony Marking the Twenty-Fifth Annual Observance of Captive Nations Week
July 19, 1983

Two visions of the world remain locked in dispute. The first believes all men are created equal by a loving God who has blessed us with freedom. Abraham Lincoln spoke for us: "No man," he said, "is good enough to govern another without the other's consent."

The second vision believes that religion is opium for the masses. It believes that eternal principles like truth, liberty, and democracy have no meaning beyond the whim of the state. And Lenin spoke for them: "It is true, that liberty is precious," he said, "so precious that it must be rationed."

Well, I'll take Lincoln's version over Lenin's, and so

will citizens of the world if they're given free choice. . . .

You are the conscience of the free world, and I appeal to you to make your voices heard. Tell [totalitarian governments]: "You may jail your people. You may seize their goods. You may ban their unions. You may bully their rabbis and dissidents. You may forbid the name of Jesus to pass their lips. But you will never destroy the love of God and freedom that burns in their hearts. They will triumph over you."

With faith as our guide, we can muster the wisdom and will to protect the deepest treasures of the human spirit—the freedom to build a better life in our time and the promise of life everlasting in his kingdom.

Aleksandr Solzhenitsyn told us, "Our entire earthly existence is but a transitional stage in the movement toward something higher, and we must not stumble and fall, for we must linger . . . on one rung of the ladder."

Meeting with Christian Religious Organizations
October 13, 1983

Many groups come to visit [the White House], but I believe yours is the first leadership group of Christian women to be welcomed to the White House in a long, long time, and I'm glad to be the one that's doing the greeting. I won't speculate why this hasn't been done before. I only know that as long as I'm president, your group and others who stand up for our Judeo-Christian values will be welcome here, because you belong here.

I can't say strongly enough what tremendous force for good you are. As life-bearers, carrying on traditions of family in the home, but also in our schools, the corporate world, in the workplace, you're teachers of cooperation, tolerance, compassion, and responsibility. No greater truth shines through than the one you live by every day: that preserving America must begin with faith in the God who has blessed our land. And we don't have the answers; he does.

Isaiah reminded us that "the Lord opens his gates and keeps in peace the nation that trusts in him." I hope you won't mind my saying I think I know you all very well. Nelle Reagan, my mother, God rest her soul, had an unshakable faith in God's goodness. And while I may not have realized it in my youth, I know now that she planted that faith very deeply in me. She made the most difficult Christian message seem very easy. And, like you, she knew you could never repay one bad deed with another. Her way was forgiveness and goodness, and both began with love.

For some time now I believe that America has been hungering for a return to spiritual values that some of us fear we've tended to forget—things like faith, families, family values—the bedrock of our nation. Thanks to the creation of new networks of faith by so many of you and your families, we're seeing more clearly again. We're remembering that freedom carries responsibilities. And we're not set free so that we can become slaves to sin.

The founding fathers believed that faith in God was the key to our being a good people and America's becoming a great nation. George Washington kissed the Bible at his inauguration. And to those who would have government separate us from religion, he had these words: "Reason and experience both forbid us to expect that national morality can prevail in exclusion of religious principle." And Ben Franklin, at the time when they were struggling with what was to be the American Constitution, finally one day said to those who were working with him, "Without God's help, we shall succeed in this political building no better than the builders of Babel." And if we ever forget that, we're lost. From that day on they opened all the constitutional meetings with prayer.

I pray that we won't lose that idea, and that's why I was motivated to proclaim or designate 1983 the Year of the Bible.

And I hope that we will also recognize the true meaning of the first amendment. Its words were meant to guarantee freedom of religion to everyone. But I believe the first amendment has been twisted to the point that freedom of religion is in danger of becoming freedom from religion.

But keep the faith. This year the Supreme Court took two big steps toward common sense.

It said that the first amendment does not prevent legislators in the Nebraska State Assembly from hiring a chaplain to open their sessions with prayer. And it said the Constitution does not prevent the State of Minnesota from giving a tax break to parents who choose private or religious schooling for their children. In both cases the court decided in favor of what our Justice Department recommended in friend of the court briefs.

Now we're making another recommendation. We believe the city of Pawtucket, Rhode Island, and for that matter, any city in America, has the right to include the Nativity scene as part of its annual Christmas performance.

Government is not supposed to wage war against God and religion, not in the United States of America. I want to see the Congress act on our constitutional amendment permitting voluntary prayer in America's schoolrooms. And here you can be our greatest help. Tell the millions of our friends to send a message of thunder from the grassroots, fill the halls of Congress with calls, with letters and telegrams—not postcards. (I understand they don't take postcards as seriously as they take letters.) And tell them, "The people have waited too long; we want action."

We think it's also time for a vote on tuition tax credits. Education's the fundamental right and responsibility of every parent. And we should remember that those who pay private tuition also pay their full share of taxes to support the public school system. Tuition tax credits would only threaten public schools if you believe that more competition, greater parental choice, and stronger local control will make our schools worse, not better.

Finally, let me just say a few words about another part of freedom that is under siege: the sanctity of human life. Either the law protects human beings, or it doesn't. When we're dealing with a handicapped child—say, a mentally retarded baby girl who needs medical care to survive, is she not entitled to the protection of the law? Will she be denied her chance for love and life because someone decides she's too weak to warrant our help, or because someone has taken it upon himself or herself to decide the quality of her life doesn't justify keeping her alive? Is that not God's decision to make? And isn't it our duty to serve even the least of these, for in so doing we serve him?

Our administration has tried to make sure the handicapped receive the respect of the law for the dignity of their lives. And the same holds true, I believe deeply, for the unborn.

Radio Address to the Nation
December 24, 1983

Some celebrate Christmas as the birthday of a great teacher and philosopher. But to other millions of us, Jesus is much more. He is divine, living assurance that God so loved the world he gave us his only begotten Son so that by believing in him and learning to love each other we could one day be together in paradise. . . .

National Religious Broadcasters Convention
January 1, 1984

If the Lord is our light, our strength, and our salvation, whom shall we fear? Of whom shall we be afraid? No matter where we live, we have a promise that can make all the difference, a promise from Jesus to soothe our sorrows, heal our hearts, and drive away our fears. He promised there will never be a dark night that does not end. Our weeping may endure for a night, but joy cometh in the morning. He promised if our hearts are true, his love will be as sure as sunlight. And by dying for us, Jesus showed how far our love should be ready to go: all the way. . . .

"For God so loved the world that he gave his only begotten Son, that whosoever believeth in him should not perish but have everlasting life."

Helping each other, believing in him, we need never be afraid. We will be part of something far more powerful, enduring, and good than all the forces here on earth. We will be a part of paradise.

Eureka College Address
February 6, 1984

In Chambers' autobiography, *Witness,* he added a sequel. Chambers marked the beginning of his personal journey away from communism on the day that he was suddenly struck by the sight of his infant daughter's ear as she sat there having breakfast. And then, he said, he realized that such intricacy, such precision could be no accident, no freak of nature. He said that while he didn't know it at the time, in that moment, God—the finger of God—had touched his forehead.

And that is why Chambers would write that faith, not economics, is the central problem of our age and that "the crisis of the western world exists to the degree in which it is indifferent to God." The western world does not know it, but it already possesses the answer to this problem, he said, provided that its "faith in God and the freedom he enjoins" is as great as communism's belief in material power.

Chambers' story represents a generation's disenchantment with statism and its return to eternal truths and fundamental values. And if there is one thought I would leave with you today, it is this: For all the momentous change of the last fifty years, it is still the great civilized truths, values of family, work, neighborhood, and religion that fuel America's technological and material progress and put the spark to our enduring passion for freedom.

We're lucky to live in a time when these traditional values and faith in the future—this sense of hope—has been reawakened in our country.

Conservative Political Action Conference
March 2, 1984

Fellow citizens, fellow conservatives, our time has come again. This is our moment. Let us unite, shoulder to shoulder, behind one mighty banner for freedom. And let us go forward from here not with some faint hope that our cause is not yet lost; let us go forward confident that the American people share our values, and that together we will be victorious.

And in those moments when we grow tired, when our struggle seems hard, remember what Eric Liddell, Scotland's Olympic champion runner, said in *Chariots of Fire*. He said, "So where does the power come from to see the race to its end? From within. God made me for a purpose, and I will run for his pleasure."

If we trust in him, keep his work, and live our lives for his pleasure, he'll give us the power we need—power to fight the good fight, to finish the race, and to keep the faith.

I think America is better off than we were three years ago because we've stopped placing our faith in more government programs. We're restoring our faith in the greatest resource this nation has—the mighty spirit of free people under God.

National Association of Evangelicals Convention
March 6, 1984

There was a minister who put his [sermon] text on the pulpit a half an hour before every service. And one Sunday a smart aleck hid the last page. And the minister preached powerfully, but when he got to the words, "So Adam said to Eve," he was horrified to discover that the final sheet was gone. And riffling through the other pages, he stalled for time by repeating, "So Adam said to Eve"—and then in a low voice he said, "There seems to be a missing leaf. . . ."

Any serious look at our history shows that from the first, the people of our country were deeply imbued with faith. Indeed, many of the first settlers came for the express purpose of worshiping in freedom. The historian Samuel Morison wrote of one such group, "doubting nothing and fearing no man, [they] undertook to set all crooked ways straight and create a new heaven and new earth. If they were not permitted to do that in England, [they] would find some other place to establish [their] city of God." Well, that other place was this broad and open land we call America.

The debates over independence and the records of the Constitutional Convention make it clear that the founding fathers were sustained by their faith in God. In the Declaration of Independence itself, Thomas Jefferson wrote that all men are " . . . endowed by their Creator with certain unalienable rights. . . ." And it was George Washington who said, "Of all the dispositions and habits which lead to political prosperity, Religion and Morality are indispensable supports."

So, the record is clear. The first Americans proclaimed their freedom because they believed God himself had granted their liberty prayerfully, avidly seeking and humbly accepting God's blessing on their new land.

For decades, America remained a deeply religious country, thanking God in peacetime and turning to him in moments of crisis. During the Civil War, perhaps our nation's darkest hour, Abraham Lincoln said, "I have been driven many times upon my knees by the conviction that I had nowhere else to go." Believe me, no one can serve in this office without understanding and believing exactly what he said.

During World War II, . . . a rally to promote war bonds that was held at Madison Square Garden in New York. The rally featured the great figures from government; great stars of the theater entertained the audience, and many times those people proclaimed that God was on our side. And then . . . a fifty-four-dollar-a-month buck private spoke nine words that no one there that day will ever forget. His name was Joe Louis—yes, the Joe Louis who had come from the cotton fields to become the world heavyweight prizefighting champion. Now this fifty-four-dollar-a-month private walked out to center stage after all those other celebrities had been there, and he said, "I know we'll win, because *we're* on *God's* side." There was a moment of silence, and then that crowd nearly took the roof off.

During the civil rights struggles of the fifties and early sixties, millions worked for equality in the name of their Creator. Civil rights leaders like Dr. Martin Luther King based all their efforts on the claim that black or white, each of us is a child of God. And they stirred our nation to the very depths of it soul.

And so it has been through most of our history. All our material wealth and all our influence have been built on our faith in God and the bedrock values that follow from that faith. The great French philosopher, Alexis de Tocqueville, 150 years ago is said to have observed that America is great because America is good. And if she ever ceases to be good, she will cease to be great.

Well, in recent years, we must admit, America did seem to lose her religious and moral bearings, to forget that faith and values are what made us good and great.

We saw the signs all around us. Years ago, pornography, while available, was sold mostly under the counter. By the mid-seventies it was available virtually on every magazine rack in every drugstore or shop in the land. Drug abuse used to be confined to limited numbers of adults. During the sixties and seventies, it spread through the nation like a fever, affecting children as well as adults and involving drugs that were once unheard of, drugs like LSD and PCP, ironically nicknamed "angel dust."

But perhaps most important, years ago, the American family was still the basic building block of our society. But then families too often found themselves penalized by government taxation, welfare policies that were spinning out of control, and the social mores of our country that were being undermined. Liberal attitudes viewed promiscuity as acceptable, even stylish. Indeed, the word itself was replaced by a new term, "sexually active." And in the media, what we once thought of as a sacred expression of love was often portrayed as something casual and cheap.

Between 1970 and 1980, the number of two-parent families dropped while the number of single-parent families almost doubled. Teenage pregnancies increased significantly. And although total births declined during the decade between 1970 and 1980, the number of illegitimate births rose about a quarter of a million.

At the same time that social standards seemed to be dissolving, our economic and governmental institutions were in disarray. Big taxing and spending had led to soaring interest rates and inflation. Our defenses had grown weak. Public officials at the highest levels openly spoke of a national malaise. All over the world America had become known not for strength and resolve, but for vacillation and self-doubt. It seemed for a season as though our nation was in permanent decline and that any sense of justice, self-discipline, and duty was ebbing out of our public life.

But the Almighty who gave us this great land also gave us free will, the power under God to choose our own destiny. The American people decided to put a stop to that long decline, and today our country is seeing a rebirth of freedom and faith, a great national renewal. As I said in my State of the Union address, "America is back. . . ."

We've begun tackling one problem after another. We've knocked inflation down, and we can keep it down. The prime rate is about half what it was when our administration took office. All across the country, a powerful economic recovery is gaining strength. As we've begun rebuilding our defenses in the name of freedom, morale in the military has soared. And once again, America is respected throughout the world as a great force for freedom and peace.

But this renewal is more than material. America has begun a spiritual awakening. Faith and hope are being restored. Americans are turning back to God. Church attendance is up. Audiences for religious books and broadcasts are growing. On college campuses, students have stopped shunning religion and started going to church. As Harvard theologian Harvey Cox put it, "Rather than the cynical, careerist types who supposedly have filled the campuses, I see young people who are intensely interested in moral issues, in religious history and beliefs."

One of my favorite Bible quotations comes from II Chronicles: " . . . if my people who are called by my name humble themselves and pray and seek my face, and turn from their wicked ways, then will I hear from heaven, and forgive their sin and heal their land." Today, Americans from Maine to California are seeking his face. And I do believe that he has begun to heal our blessed land.

As this special awakening gathers strength, we must remember that many in good faith will hold other views. Let us pledge to conduct ourselves with generosity, tolerance, and openness toward all. We must respect the rights and views of every American, because we're unshakably committed to democratic values. Our Maker would have it no less.

So, please use your pulpits to denounce racism, anti-Semitism, and all ethnic or religious intolerance as evils, and let us make it clear that our values must not restrict, but liberate the human spirit in thought and in deed.

You may remember, but I'm sure you don't agree with, a very cynical quote that got wide circulation, from H. L. Mencken. He said puritanism "is the haunting fear that someone, somewhere, may be happy."

Well, some suspect that today's spiritual awakening reflects such narrow-mindedness. We must show that faith and traditional values are the things that give life human dignity, warmth, vitality, and yes, laughter and joy.

Sometimes we all must think when we look at ourselves—the Lord must have a sense of humor.

Now, although millions of Americans have already done so much to put our national life back on the firm foundation of faith and traditional values, we still have far to go.

In foreign affairs I believe there are two fundamental tasks that we must perform. First, we must make certain our own country is strong, so we can go on holding out the hope of freedom for all the world. When I took office, I made rebuilding our defenses a top priority. Although we still have a great deal to do, we've already made dramatic headway. And since American forces are the cornerstone in the global defense of liberty, that's good news for all the world.

Second, in this age when electronics beam messages around the globe, we must keep telling the truth, including the truth about the difference between free and totalitarian societies.

This month it will be my honor to award a posthumous medal of honor—a Medal of Freedom, I should say—to Whittaker Chambers, a man of courage and wisdom. Chambers understood the struggle between totalitarianism and the West. He, himself, had turned to communism out of a sense of idealism in which he thought that might be the answer.

I don't know whether you've ever read his [story about how] he first began to awaken. They had a new baby, a little girl. And he was looking at her one morning as she sat in her high chair. And he said he found himself looking at the delicate convolutions of that tiny ear. And that was when he said to himself, "That cannot be just an accident, a freak of nature." And he said he may not have realized it at the moment, but he knows that in that moment, God had laid his finger on his forehead.

When men try to live in a world without God, it's only too easy for them to forget the rights that God bestows—too easy to suppress freedom of speech, to build walls to keep their countrymen, to jail dissidents, and to put great thinkers in mental wards. We will deal with the Communist world as we must with a great power: by negotiating with it, from strength and in good faith.

And if the new Soviet leadership is willing, we will renew our efforts to ease tensions between East and West. While we will never accept for ourselves their system, we will never stop praying that the leaders, like so many of their own people, might come to know the liberating nature of faith in God. . . .

Here at home, I believe there are three basic tasks that we must accomplish. First, we must do our duty to generations not yet born. We cannot proclaim the noble ideal that human life is sacred, then turn our backs on the taking of some 4,000 unborn children's lives every day. [Abortion] as a means of birth control must stop. . . .

Second, we must restore education in basic values to America's schools. Since our administration put education at the top of the national agenda, we've seen a grassroots revolution that promises to strengthen every school in the country. Across the land, parents, teachers, school administrators, state and local officeholders have begun to work to improve the fundamentals—not frills in the curriculum, but basic teaching and learning. As this great educational reform takes place, we must make certain that we not only improve instruction in math and science, but in justice, religion, discipline, and liberty, for to guide America into the twenty-first century, our children will need not only technical skills but wisdom. . . .

And third, school prayer. From the early days of the American colonies, prayer in schools was practiced and revered as an important tradition. Indeed, for nearly two centuries of our history it was considered a natural expression of our religious freedom. Then in 1962 the Supreme Court declared school prayer illegal. Well, I firmly believe that the loving God who has blessed our land and made us a good and caring people should never have been expelled from America's classrooms. And the country agrees. Polls show that by a majority of 80 percent, the American people want prayer back in our schools.

We stand on firm historical and constitutional ground. During the constitutional convention, Benjamin Franklin rose to say, "The longer I live, the more convincing proofs I see that God governs in the affairs of men. Without His concurring aid, we shall succeed in this political building no better than the builders of Babel." And he asked, "Have we now forgotten this powerful Friend? Or do we imagine we no longer need His assistance?" And then Franklin moved that the convention begin its daily deliberations by asking for the assistance of Almighty God.

Today, prayer remains a vital part of American public life. The Congress begins each day with prayer, and the Supreme Court begins each sitting with an invocation. Now, I just have to believe that if the members of Congress and the Justices can acknowledge the Almighty, our children can too. . . .

Saint Paul wrote a verse that I've always cherished, "Now abide faith, hope, love, these three: but the greatest of these is love." May we have faith in our God and in all the good that we can do with his help. May we stand firm in the hope of making America all that she can be— a nation of opportunity and prosperity and a force for peace and good will among nations. And may we remain steadfast in our love for this green and gentle land and the freedom that she offers.

FIVE

IF MY PEOPLE . . .

The President's Statements on Prayer

If my people will humble themselves and pray, and search for me, and turn from their wicked ways, I will hear them from heaven and forgive their sins and heal their land (II Chronicles 7:14, TLB).

Inaugural Address
January 20, 1981

I'm told that tens of thousands of prayer meetings are being held on this day, and for that I'm deeply grateful. We are a nation under God, and I believe God intended for us to be free. It would be fitting and good, I think, if on each Inaugural Day in future years it should be declared a day of prayer.

National Day of Prayer Proclamation
March 19, 1981

Our nation's motto—"In God We Trust"—was not chosen lightly. It reflects a basic recognition that there is a divine authority in the universe to which the nation owes homage.

Throughout our history Americans have put their faith in God and no one can doubt that we have been blessed for it. The earliest settlers of this land came in search of religious freedom. Landing on a desolate shoreline, they established a spiritual foundation that has served us ever since.

It was the hard work of our people, the freedom they enjoyed and their faith in God that built this country and made it the envy of the world. In all of our great cities and towns evidence of the faith of our people is found: houses of worship of every denomination are among the oldest structures.

While never willing to bow to a tyrant, our forefathers were always willing to get to their knees before God. When catastrophe threatened, they turned to God for deliverance. When the harvest was bountiful, the first thought was thanksgiving to God.

Prayer is today as powerful a force in our nation as it has ever been. We as a nation should never forget this source of strength. And while recognizing that the freedom to choose a godly path is the essence of liberty, as a nation we cannot but hope that more of our citizens would, through prayer, come into a closer relationship with their Maker.

Recognizing our great heritage, the Congress, by Joint Resolution approved April 17, 1952 , has called upon the president to set aside a suitable day each year as a National Day of Prayer.

Now, therefore, I, Ronald Reagan, President of the United States of America, do hereby proclaim Thursday, May 7, 1981, National Day of Prayer. On that day I ask all who believe to join with me in giving thanks to Almighty God for the blessings he has bestowed on this land and the protection he afforts us as a people. Let us as a nation join together before God, fully aware of the trials that lie ahead and the need, yes, the necessity, for divine guidance. With unshakable faith in God and the liberty which is heritage, we as a free nation will surely survive and prosper.

National Prayer Breakfast
February 4, 1982

You know, in one of the conflicts that was going on throughout the past year when views were held deeply on both
sides of the debate, I recall talking to one senator who came
into my office. We both deeply believed what it was we
were espousing, but we were on opposite sides. And when
we finished talking, as he rose he said, "I'm going out of
here and do some praying." And I said, "Well, if you get
a busy signal, it's me there ahead of you."

White House Ceremony in Observance of National Day of Prayer
May 6, 1982

Many of you are leaders in your faith; others are active in
your communities, your professions, or are among our
elected representatives. But all of us are here with a common
purpose: to observe a National Day of Prayer, a tradition
that was begun by the Continental Congress—that the first
Thursday of May would be such a day.

Prayer has sustained our people in crisis, strengthened
us in times of challenge, and guided us through our daily
lives since the first settlers came to this continent. Our forebearers came not for gold, but mainly in search of God
and the freedom to worship in their own way.

We've been a free people living under the law, with
faith in our Maker and in our future. I've said before that
the most sublime picture in American history is of George
Washington on his knees in the snow at Valley Forge. That
image personifies a people who know that it's not enough

to depend on our own courage and goodness; we must also seek help from God, our Father and Preserver. . . .

The French philosopher Alexis de Tocqueville, visiting America a hundred and fifty years ago, marveled at Americans because they understood that a free people must also be a religious people. "Despotism," he wrote, "may be able to do without faith, but freedom cannot."

Today, prayer is still a powerful force in America, and our faith in God is a mighty source of strength. Our Pledge of Allegiance states that we are "one nation under God," and our currency bears the motto, "In God We Trust."

The morality and values such faith implies are deeply embedded in our national character. Our country embraces those principles by design, and we abandon them at our peril. Yet in recent years, well-meaning Americans in the name of freedom have taken freedom away. For the sake of religious tolerance, they've forbidden religious practice in our public classrooms. The law of this land has effectively removed prayer from our classrooms.

How can we hope to retain our freedom through the generations if we fail to teach our young that our liberty springs from an abiding faith in our Creator?

Thomas Jefferson once said, "Almighty God created the mind free." But current interpretation of our Constitution holds that the minds of our children cannot be free to pray to God in public schools. No one will ever convince me that a moment of voluntary prayer will harm a child or threaten a school or state. But I think it can strengthen our faith in a Creator who alone has the power to bless America.

One of my favorite passages in the Bible is the promise God gives us in II Chronicles: "If my people, which are called by my name, shall humble themselves and pray, and search for me, and turn from their wicked ways, then will I hear them from heaven and forgive their sins and heal their land."

That promise is the hope of America and of all our people.

Because of my faith in that promise, I'm particularly pleased to be able to tell you today that this administration will soon submit to the United States Congress a proposal to amend our Constitution to allow our children to pray in school. No one must ever be forced or coerced or pressured to take part in any religious exercise, but neither should the government forbid religious practice. The amendment we'll propose will restore the right to pray.

I thank you all for coming here today and for the good work that you do for our people, our country, and our God every day of the year. But I also hope that I can count on your help in the days and months ahead as we work for passage of this amendment.

Changing the Constitution is a mammoth task. It would never be easy. But in this case, I believe we can restore a freedom that our Constitution was always meant to protect. I have never believed that the oft-quoted amendment was supposed to protect us from religion. It was to protect religion from government tyranny.

Together, let us take up the challenge to reawaken America's religious and moral heart, recognizing that a deep and abiding faith in God is the rock upon which this great nation was founded.

Administration Briefing, Q & A Session with Editors from the Midwest
May 10, 1982

Question: Mr. President, why is a constitutional prayer amendment necessary when the Supreme Court only outlawed officially sponsored prayers, not silent prayers or meditation periods?

The President: Well, because that Supreme Court decision has been taken and interpreted by many who fear running counter to the law in such a way that we're finding it impossible to have Christmas ceremonies in schools anymore.

At first, the decision in most schools was, "Well, as long as you stick to Santa Claus and a Christmas tree, yes, you can have a Christmas party or ceremony." But if you do anything with the creche or observe whose birthday it is, then that is against their taking of the Constitution. And then more recently, we have found in some of our larger cities that the school boards have decided that Santa Claus is so associated with the holy holiday that, therefore, we can't have Santa Claus anymore as part of the school services.

What we're saying is that the first amendment, frankly, [was not] properly interpreted. The first amendment is to protect not government from religion, but religion from government tyranny. It says that the government will neither respect nor obstruct—or will neither institute nor obstruct religious practice. And the prayers, I think, would obviously have to be nonsectarian so that you are not showing favor to one particular religion or another. And I know that New York State had proposed a nonsectarian prayer that would meet all of the needs.

I think what most people in this country [think]—and the polls show that it is overwhelming, the percentage of people who want prayer restored—is the idea that by doing away with it, it was almost as if there was an anti-religious bias. It was as if saying to the children that this is no longer important. And yet we refer to ours as a country under God. It says "In God We Trust" on our coins. They open the Congress sessions with a chaplain. I've never been sure whether he prays for the Congress or for the nation.

A Proposed Constitutional Amendment on Prayer in School
May 17, 1982

I have attached for your consideration a proposed constitutional amendment to restore the simple freedom of our citizens to offer prayer in our public schools and institutions. The public expression through prayer of our faith in God is a fundamental part of our American heritage and a privilege which should not be excluded by law from any American school, public or private.

One hundred fifty years ago, Alexis de Tocqueville found that all Americans believed that religious faith was indispensable to the maintenance of their republican institutions. Today, I join with the people of this nation in acknowledging this basic truth, that our liberty springs from and depends upon an abiding faith in God. This has been clear from the time of George Washington, who stated in his farewell address: Of all the dispositions and habits which lead to political prosperity, religion and morality are indispensable supports . . . And let us with caution indulge the supposition that morality can be maintained without religion . . . . Reason and experience both forbid us to expect that national morality can prevail in exclusion of religious principle.

Nearly every president since Washington has proclaimed a day of public prayer and thanksgiving to acknowledge the many favors of Almighty God. We have acknowledged God's guidance on our coinage, in our national anthem, and in the Pledge of Allegiance. As the Supreme Court has stated: "We are a religious people whose institutions presuppose a Supreme Being."

The founders of our nation and the framers of the First Amendment did not intend to forbid public prayer. On the contrary, prayer has been part of our public assemblies since Benjamin Franklin's eloquent request that prayer be observed by the Constitutional Convention:

> I have lived, Sir, a long time, and the longer I live, the more convincing proofs I see of this truth—that God governs in the affairs of men . . . I also believe that without his concurring aid we shall succeed in this political building no better than the builders of Babel: We shall be divided by our little partial local interests; our projects will be confounded, and we ourselves shall become a reproach and bye-word down to future ages. . . . I therefore beg leave to move— that henceforth prayers imploring the assistance of Heaven, and its blessings on our deliberations, be held in this Assembly every morning before we proceed to business. . . .

Just as Benjamin Franklin believed it was beneficial for the Constitutional Convention to begin each day's work with a prayer, I believe that it would be beneficial for our children to have an opportunity to begin each school day in the same manner. Since the law has been construed to prohibit this, I believe that the law should be changed. It is time for the people, through their Congress and the state legislatures, to act, using the means afforded them by the Constitution.

The amendment I propose will remove the bar to school prayer established by the Supreme Court and allow prayer back in our schools. However, the amendment also expressly affirms the right of anyone to refrain from prayer. The amendment will allow communities to determine for themselves whether prayer should be permitted in their public schools and to allow individuals to decide for themselves whether they wish to participate in prayer.

I am confident that such an amendment will be quickly adopted, for the vast majority of our people believe there is a need for prayer in our public schools and institutions. I look forward to working with Congress to achieve the passage of this amendment.

Radio Address to the Nation
September 18, 1982

At every crucial turning point in our history Americans have faced and overcome great odds, strengthened by spiritual faith. The Plymouth settlers triumphed over hunger, disease, and a cruel Northern wilderness because, in the words of William Bradford, "They knew they were Pilgrims, so they committed themselves to the will of God and resolved to proceed."

George Washington knelt in prayer at Valley Forge and in the darkest days of our struggle for independence said that "the fate of unborn milions will now depend, under God, on the courage and conduct of this army."

Thomas Jefferson, perhaps the wisest of our founding fathers, had no doubt about the source from which our cause was derived. "The God who gave us life," he declared, "gave us liberty."

And nearly a century later, in the midst of a tragic and at times seemingly hopeless Civil War, Abraham Lincoln vowed that "this nation, under God, shall have a new birth of freedom."

It's said that prayer can move mountains. Well, it's certainly moved the hearts and minds of Americans in their times of trial and helped them to achieve a society that, for all its imperfections, is still the envy of the world and the last, best hope of mankind.

And just as prayer has helped us as a nation, it helps us as individuals. In nearly all our lives, there are moments when our prayers and the prayers of our friends and loved ones help to see us through and keep [us] on the right path. In fact, prayer is one of the few things in the world that hurts no one and sustains the spirit of millions.

The founding fathers felt this so strongly that they enshrined the principle of freedom of religion in the first amendment of the Constitution. The purpose of that amendment was to protect religion from the interference of government and to guarantee, in its own words, "the free exercise of religion."

Yet today we're told that to protect that first amendment, we must suppress prayer and expel God from our children's classrooms. In one case, a court has ruled against the right of children to say grace in their own school cafeteria before they had lunch. A group of children who sought, on their initiative and with their parents' approval, to begin the school day with a one-minute prayer meditation have been forbidden to do so. And some students who wanted to join in prayer or religious study on school property, even outside of regular class hours, have been banned from doing so.

A few people have even objected to prayers being said in the Congress. That's just plain wrong. The Constitution was never meant to prevent people from praying; its declared purpose was to protect their freedom to pray.

The time has come for this Congress to give a majority of American families what they want for their children—the firm assurance that children can hold voluntary prayers

66

in their schools just as the Congress, itself, begins each of its daily sessions with an opening prayer.

With this in mind, last May I proposed to the Congress a measure that declares once and for all that nothing in the Constitution prohibits prayer in public schools or institutions. It also states that no person shall be required by government to participate in prayer who does not want to. So, everyone's rights—believers and nonbelievers alike—are protected by our voluntary prayer measure.

I'm sorry to say that so far the Congress has failed to vote on the issue of school prayer. Just this week, however, I asked Senate Majority Leader Howard Baker to bring this measure to a floor vote. I'm happy to say he told me he'll do everything he can to accomplish this. However, passage requires a vote by the House of Representatives as well. So, I call on the House leadership to make an equal effort.

Today, on one of the holiest days of one of our great religious faiths, I urge the members of the Congress to set aside their differences and act on this simple, fair, and long-overdue measure to help make us "one nation under God" again.

School Prayer Day; Candle-Lighting Ceremony
September 25, 1982

Unfortunately, in the last two decades we've experienced an onslaught of such twisted logic that if Alice were visiting America, she might think she'd never left Wonderland.

We're told that it somehow violates the rights of others to permit students in school who desire to pray to do so. Clearly this infringes on the freedom of those who choose to pray, the freedom taken for granted since the time of our Founding Fathers. . . . Now, no one is suggesting that others should be forced into any religious activity, but to prevent those who believe in God from expressing their faith is an outrage. And the relentless drive to eliminate God from our schools can and should be stopped. . . . We can and must respect the rights of those who are nonbelievers, but we must not cut ourselves off from this indispensable source of strength and guidance.

National Day of Prayer, 1983
January 27, 1983

Prayer is the mainspring of the American spirit, a fundamental tenet of our people since before the Republic was founded. A year before the Declaration of Independence, in 1775, the Continental Congress proclaimed the first National Day of Prayer as the initial positive action they asked of every colonist.

Two hundred years ago in 1783, the Treaty of Paris officially ended the long, weary Revolutionary War during which a National Day of Prayer had been proclaimed every spring for eight years. When peace came, the National Day of Prayer was forgotten. For almost half a century, as the nation grew in power and wealth, we put aside this deepest expression of American belief—our national dependence on the providence of God.

It took the tragedy of the Civil War to restore a National Day of Prayer. As Abraham Lincoln said, "Intoxicated with unbroken success, we have become too self-sufficient to feel the necessity of redeeming and preserving grace, too proud to pray to the God that made us."

Revived as an annual observance by Congress in 1952,

the National Day of Prayer has become a great unifying force for our citizens who come from all the great religions of the world. Prayer unites people. This common expression of reverence heals and brings us together as a nation, and we pray it may one day bring renewed respect for God to all the peoples of the world.

From General Washington's struggle at Valley Forge to the present, this nation has fervently sought and received divine guidance as it pursued the course of history. This occasion provides our nation with an opportunity to further recognize the source of our blessings, and to seek his help for the challenges we face today and in the future.

National Prayer Breakfast
February 3, 1983

I know that at times all of us—I do—feel that perhaps in our prayers we ask for too much. And then there are those other times when we feel that something isn't important enough to bother God with it. Maybe we should let him decide those things.

The war correspondent Marguerite Higgins, who received the Pulitzer Prize for International Reporting because of her coverage of the Korean war, among all her writings had an account of the Fifth Company of marines who were part of an 18,000-man force that was in combat with a hundred thousand of the enemy. And she described an incident that took place early, just after dawn on a very cold morning. It was forty-two degrees below zero. And the weary marines, half frozen, stood by their dirty, mud-covered trucks, eating their breakfast from tin cans.

One huge marine was eating cold beans with a trench

knife. His clothes were frozen stiff as a board; his face was covered with a heavy beard and crusted with mud. And one of the little group of war correspondents who were on hand went up to him and said, "If I were God and could grant you anything you wished, what would you most like?" And the marine stood there for a moment, looking down at that cold tin of beans, and then he raised his head and said, "Give me tomorrow."

Christian Religious Organizations
October 13, 1983

Hardly a day goes by that I'm not told—sometimes in letters and sometimes by people that I meet and perfect strangers—that they're praying for me. Well, thanks to [my mother] Nelle Reagan, I believe in intercessory prayer. And I know that those prayers are giving me strength that I otherwise would not possess.

National Day of Prayer Proclamation
December 14, 1983

In 1787, a then elderly Benjamin Franklin said to George Washington as he presided over the Constitutional Convention, "I have lived, sir, a long time, and the longer I live the more convincing proofs I see of this truth, that God governs in the affairs of men. And if a sparrow cannot fall to the ground without his notice, is it probable that an empire can rise without his aid?"

With these words, Mr. Franklin called upon the Convention to open each day with prayer, and from the birth of our Republic, prayer has been vital to the whole fabric of American life.

As we crossed and settled a continent, built a nation in freedom, and endured war and critical struggles to become the leader of the free world and a sentinel of liberty, we repeatedly turned to our Maker for strength and guidance in achieving the awesome tasks before us.

From the poignancy of General Washington's legendary prayer in the snow at Valley Forge to the dangerous times in which we live today, our leaders and the people of this nation have called upon Divine Providence and trusted in God's wisdom to guide us through the challenges we have faced as a people and a nation.

Whether at the landing of our forebearers in New England and Virginia, the ordeal of the Revolutionary War, the stormy days of binding the thirteen colonies into one country, the Civil War, or other moments of trial over the years, we have turned to God for his help. As we are told in II Chronicles 7:14: "If my people, will humble themselves and pray, and search for me, and turn from their wicked ways, I will hear them from heaven and forgive their sins and heal their land."

By Joint Resolution of the Congress approved April 17, 1952, the recognition of a particular day set aside each year as a National Day of Prayer has become part of our unification as a great nation. This is a day on which the people of the United States are invited to turn to God in prayer and meditation in places of worship, in groups, and as individuals. Since 1952, each president has proclaimed annually a National Day of Prayer, resuming the tradition started by the Continental Congress.

Now, therefore, I, Ronald Reagan, President of the United States of America, do hereby proclaim Thursday, May 3, 1984, as National Day of Prayer. I call upon the citizens of this great nation to gather together on that day in homes and places of worship to pray, each after his or her own manner, for unity of the hearts of all mankind.

State of Union Address
January 25, 1984

Each day your members observe a 200-year-old tradition meant to signify America is one nation under God. I must ask: If you can begin your day with a member of the clergy standing right here leading you in prayer, then why can't freedom to acknowledge God be enjoyed again by children in every school room across this land?

America was founded by people who believed that God was their rock of safety. He is ours. I recognize we must be cautious in claiming that God is on our side, but I think it's all right to keep asking if we're on his side.

National Religious Broadcasters
January 30, 1984

I know one thing I'm sure most of us agree on: God, source of all knowledge, should never have been expelled from our children's classrooms. The great majority of our people support voluntary prayer in schools.

We hear of cases where courts say it is dangerous to allow students to meet in Bible study or prayer clubs. And then there was the case of that kindergarten class that was reciting a verse. They said, "We thank you for the flowers so sweet. We thank you for the food we eat. We thank you for the birds that sing. We thank you, God, for everything." A court of appeals ordered them to stop. They were supposedly violating the Constitution of the United States.

Well, Teddy Roosevelt told us, "The American people are slow to wrath, but when their wrath is once kindled, it burns like a consuming flame."

I think Americans are getting angry. I think they have

a message, and Congress better listen. We are a government of, by, and for the people. And people want a constitutional amendment making it unequivocally clear our children can hold voluntary prayer in every school across this land. If we could get God and discipline back in our schools, maybe we could get drugs and violence out. . . .

National Prayer Breakfast
February 2, 1984

We all in this room, I know, and we know many millions more everywhere, turn to God in prayer, believe in the power and the spirit of prayer. And yet, so often, we direct our prayers to those problems that are immediate to us, knowing that he has promised his help to us when we turn to him. And yet, in a world today that is so torn with strife where the divisions seem to be increasing . . . I wonder if we have ever thought about the greatest tool that we have. The power of prayer and God's help.

If you could add together the power of prayer of the people just in this room, what would be its megatonnage? And have we maybe been neglecting . . . the broader [sense] in which we pray to be forgiven for the animus we feel toward someone in perhaps a legitimate dispute, and at the same time recognize that while the dispute will go on, we have to realize that the other individual is a child of God even as we are. . . .

This power of prayer can be illustrated by a story that goes back to the fourth century—the Asian monk living in a little remote village, spending most of his time in prayer or tending the garden from which he obtained his sustenance. . . . One day he thought he heard the voice of God telling him to go to Rome. And believing that he had heard, he set out. Weeks and weeks later, he arrived there, having traveled most of the way on foot.

It was at a time of a festival in Rome. They were celebrating a triumph over the Goths. He followed a crowd into the Colosseum, and then, there in the midst of this great crowd, he saw the gladiators come forth, stand before the Emperor, and say, "We who are about to die salute you." And he realized they were going to fight to the death for the entertainment of the crowds. He cried out, "In the name of Christ, stop!" And his voice was lost in the tumult there in the great Colosseum.

And as the games began, he made his way down through the crowd and climbed over the wall and dropped to the floor of the arena. Suddenly the crowds saw this scrawny little figure making his way out to the gladiators and saying, over and over again, "In the name of Christ, stop." And they thought it was part of the entertainment, and at first they were amused. But then, when they realized it wasn't, they grew belligerent and angry. And as he was pleading with the gladiators, "In the name of Christ, stop," one of them plunged his sword into his body. And as he fell to the sand of the arena in death, his last words were, "In the name of Christ, stop."

And suddenly, a strange thing happened. The gladiators stood looking at this tiny form lying in the sand. A silence fell over the Colosseum. And then, someplace up in the upper tiers, an individual made his way to an exit and left, and the others began to follow. And in the dead silence, everyone left the Colosseum. That was the last battle to the death between gladiators in the Roman Colosseum. Never again did anyone kill or did men kill each other for the entertainment of the crowd.

One tiny voice that could hardly be heard above the tumult. "In the name of Christ, stop." It is something we could be saying to each other throughout the world today.

Now, several days ago, while I was very concerned about what I was going to say here today, . . . I received through diplomatic channels a message from far out across the Pacific. Sometime ago, our ambassador presented to General Romulo of the Philippines the American Medal of Freedom. Not only had he been a great friend of the United States in our time of war, but then he had spent seventeen years as an ambassador here in Washington, from his country to ours. And for whatever reason, he sent this message of thanks to me for the medal that had been given, and then included the farewell statement that he had made when he left Washington, left this country, after those seventeen years.

And I had to confess, I had never been aware that there had been such a farewell message, and I'm quite sure that many of you hadn't. And so, I'm going to share it with you. I think it fits what we're talking about today. He said, "I am going home, America. For seventeen years, I have enjoyed your hospitality, visited every one of your fifty States. I can say I know you well. I admire and love America. It is my second home. What I have to say now in parting is both tribute and warning.

"Never forget, Americans, that yours is a spiritual country. Yes, I know you're a practical people. Like others, I've marveled at your factories, your skyscrapers, and your arsenals. But underlying everything else is the fact that America began as a God-loving, God-fearing, God-worshiping people, knowing that there is a spark of the divine in each one of us. It is this respect for the dignity of the human spirit which keeps America invincible.

"May you always endure and, as I say again in parting, thank you, America, and farewell. May God keep you always, and may you always keep God."

National Association of Secondary School Principals Meeting
February 7, 1984

The God who blessed us with life, gave us knowledge, and made us a good and caring people should never have been expelled from America's schools.

As we struggle to teach our children the fundamental values we hold so dear, we dare not forget that our civilization was built by men and women who placed their faith in a loving God. If the Congress can begin each day with a moment of prayer and meditation, so then can our sons and daughters.

National Day of Prayer, 1984 Proclamation
February 12, 1984

National prayer is deeply rooted in our American heritage. From the earliest days of our Republic, Americans have asked God to hear their prayers in times of sorrow and crisis and in times of bounty.

The first National Day of Prayer was proclaimed in 1775 by the Second Continental Congress. As thousands gathered in prayer in places of worship and encampments throughout the new land, the dispersed colonists found a new spirit of unity and resolve in this remarkable expression of public faith. For the first time, Americans of every religious persuasion prayed as one, asking for divine guidance in their quest for liberty and justice. Ever since, Americans have shared a special sense of destiny as a nation dedicated under God to the cause of liberty for all men.

Through the storms of Revolution, Civil War, and the great World Wars, as well as during times of disillusionment and disarray, the nation has turned to God in prayer for deliverance. We thank him for answering our call, for, surely, he has. As a nation, we have been richly blessed with his love and generosity.

Radio Address to the Nation
February 25, 1984

From the early days of the colonies, prayer in school was practiced and revered as an important tradition. Indeed, for nearly 200 years of our nation's history, it was considered a natural expression of our religious freedom. But in 1962, the Supreme Court handed down a controversial decision prohibiting prayer in public schools.

Sometimes I can't help but feel the first amendment is being turned on its head. Ask yourselves: Can it really be true that the first amendment can permit Nazis and Ku Klux Klansmen to march on public property, advocate the extermination of people of the Jewish faith and the subjugation of blacks, while the same amendment forbids our children from saying a prayer in school?

When a group of students at the Guilderland High School in Albany, New York, sought to use an empty classroom for voluntary prayer meetings, the Second Circuit Court of Appeals said no. The court thought it might be dangerous because students might be coerced into praying if they saw the football captain or student body president participating in prayer meetings. . . .

Up to 80 percent of the American people support voluntary prayer. They understand what the founding fathers intended. The first amendment of the Constitution was not written to protect the people from religion; that amendment was written to protect religion from government tyranny.

The amendment says, "Congress shall make no law respecting an establishment of religion or prohibiting the free exercise thereof." What could be more clear?

The act that established our public school system called for public education to see that our children learned about religion and morality. References to God can be found in the Mayflower Compact of 1620, the Declaration of Independence, the Pledge of Allegiance, and the National Anthem. Our legal tender states, "In God We Trust."

When the Constitution was being debated at the Constitutional Convention, Benjamin Franklin rose to say, "The longer I live, the more convincing proofs I see that God governs in the affairs of men. Without his concurring aid, we shall succeed in this political building no better than the builders of Babel." He asked: "Have we now forgotten this powerful Friend? Or do we imagine we no longer need His assistance?" Franklin then asked the Convention to begin its daily deliberations by asking for the assistance of Almighty God.

George Washington believed that religion was an essential pillar of a strong society. In his farewell address, he said, "Reason and experience both forbid us to expect that national morality can prevail in exclusion of religious principle." And when John Jay, the first Chief Justice of the United States Supreme Court, was asked in his dying hour if he had any farewell counsels to leave his children, Jay answered, "They have the Book."

But now we're told our children have no right to pray in school. Nonsense. The pendulum has swung too far toward intolerance against genuine religious freedom. It's time to redress the balance.

Former Supreme Court Justice Potter Stewart noted if religious exercises are held to be an impermissible activity in schools, religion is placed at an artificial and state-created disadvantage. Permission for such exercises for those who want them is necessary if the schools are truly to be neutral in the matter of religion. And a refusal to permit them is seen not as the realization of state neutrality, but rather as the establishment of a religion of secularism.

The Senate will soon vote on a constitutional amendment to permit voluntary vocal prayer in public schools. If two-thirds of the Senate aprove, then we must convince the House leadership to permit a vote on the issue. I am confident that if the Congress passes our amendment this year, then the state legislatures will do likewise, and we'll be able to celebrate a great victory for our children.

Our amendment would ensure that no child be forced to recite a prayer. Indeed, it explicitly states this. Nor would that state be allowed to compose the words of any prayer. But the courts could not forbid our children from voluntary vocal prayer in their schools. And by reasserting their liberty of free religious expression, we will be helping our children understand the diversity of America's religious beliefs and practices.

If ever there was a time for you, the good people of this country, to make your voices heard, to make the mighty power of your will the decisive force in the halls of Congress, that time is now.

School Prayer Amendment to the Constitution
March 20, 1984

I am deeply disappointed that, although a majority of the Senate voted for it, the school prayer amendment fell short of the special two-thirds majority needed to win in the Senate today.

I would like to express my heart-felt gratitude for the unprecedented outpouring of support from citizens who made their views known to their senators on this issue. And I want to thank Senators Baker, Thurmond, Helms, and Hatch for their valiant efforts to restore this revered American tradition.

This has been an important debate revealing the extent to which the freedom of religious speech has been abridged in our nation's public schools. The issue of free religious speech is not dead as a result of this vote. We have suffered a setback, but we have not been defeated. Our struggle will go on.

The courts themselves can restore a more balanced view of the first amendment, as we have seen in some recent cases. My administration will continue our efforts to allow government to accommodate prayer and religious speech by citizens in ways that do not risk an establishment of religion. I urge the Congress to consider the equal access legislation before both Houses so that voluntary student religious groups can meet on public school property on the same terms as other student groups.

SIX

THE FUTURE
WITH THE BIBLE

The President's Statements on the Bible

The grass withers, the flowers fade, but the Word of our God shall stand forever (Isaiah 40:8, TLB).

National Religious Broadcasters Convention
January 31, 1983

When Americans reach out for values of faith, family, and caring for the needy, they're saying, "We want the Word of God. We want to face the future with the Bible."

We're blessed to have its words of strength, comfort, and truth. I'm accused of being simplistic at times with some of the problems that confront us. But I've often wondered: Within the covers of that single Book are all the answers to all the problems that face us today, if we'd only look there. "The grass withereth, the flower fadeth, but the word of our God shall stand forever." It's my firm belief that the enduring values, as I say, presented in its pages have a great meaning for each of us and for our nation. The Bible can touch our hearts, order our minds, refresh our souls.

Now, I realize it's fashionable in some circles to believe that no one in government should . . . encourage others to read the Bible. . . . We're told that will violate the constitutional separation of church and state established by the founding fathers in the first amendment.

Well, it might interest those critics to know that none other than the father of our country, George Washington, kissed the Bible at his inauguration. And he also said words to the effect that there could be no real morality in a society without religion.

John Adams called it "the best book in the world." And Ben Franklin said, " . . . the longer I live, the more convincing proofs I see of this truth, that God governs in the affairs of men . . . without His concurring aid, we shall succeed in this political building no better than the builders of Babel; we shall be divided by our little, partial, local interests, our projects will be confounded, and we ourselves shall become a reproach, a bye-word down to future ages."

National Prayer Breakfast
February 3, 1983

I'm so thankful that there will always be one day in the year when people all over our land can sit down as neighbors and friends and remind ourselves of what our real task is. This task was spelled out in the Old and the New Testament. Jesus was asked, "Master, which is the great commandment in the law?" And he replied, "Thou shalt love the Lord thy God with all thy heart, and with all thy soul, and with all thy mind. This is the first and great commandment. The second is like unto it, thou shalt love thy neighbor as thyself. On these two commandments hang all the law and the prophets."

Can we resolve to reach, learn, and try to heed the greatest message ever written—God's Word and the Holy Bible? Inside its pages lie all the answers to all the problems that man has ever known.

Now, I am assuming a new position; but I should warn our friends in the loyal opposition, this new job won't require me to leave the White House. With the greatest enthusiasm, I have agreed to serve as honorary chairman for the Year of the Bible.

We think how many people in the world are imprisoned or tortured—harassed for even possessing a Bible or trying to read one. . . . In its lessons and the great wealth of its words, we find comfort, strength, wisdom, and hope. . . . We might remember something that Abraham Lincoln said over a hundred years ago: "We have forgotten the gracious hand that preserved us in peace, and multiplied and enriched and strengthened us; and we have vainly imagined, in the deceitfulness of our hearts, that all these blessings were produced by some superior wisdom and virtue of our own . . . we have become too proud to pray to the God that made us."

We face great challenges in this country, but we've faced great challenges before and conquered them. What carried us through was a willingness to seek power and protection from One much greater than ourselves, to turn back to him and to trust in his mercy. Without his help, America will not go forward.

I have a very special old Bible. And alongside a verse in the Second Book of Chronicles there are some words, handwritten, very faded by now. And, believe me, the person who wrote those words was an authority. Her name was Nelle Wilson Reagan. She was my mother. And she wrote about that verse, "A most wonderful verse for the healing of the nations."

Now, the verse that she'd marked reads: "If my people, which are called by my name, shall humble themselves, and pray, and seek my face, and turn from their wicked ways, then will I hear from heaven . . . and will heal their land."

Year of the Bible Proclamation
February 3, 1983

Of the many influences that have shaped the United States of America into a distinctive nation and people, none may be said to be more fundamental and enduring than the Bible.

Deep religious beliefs stemming from the Old and New Testaments of the Bible inspired many of the early settlers of our country, providing them with the strength, character, convictions, and faith necessary to withstand great hardship and danger in this new and rugged land. These shared beliefs helped forge a sense of common purpose among the widely dispersed colonies—a sense of community which laid the foundation for the spirit of nationhood that was to develop in later decades.

The Bible and its teachings helped form the basis for the founding fathers' abiding belief in the inalienable rights of the individual, rights which they found implicit in the Bible's teachings of the inherent worth and dignity of each individual. This same sense of man patterned the convictions of those who framed the English system of law inherited by our own nation, as well as the ideals set forth in the Declaration of Independence and the Constitution.

For centuries, the Bible's emphasis on compassion and love for our neighbor has inspired institutional and governmental expressions of benevolent outreach such as private charity, the establishment of schools and hospitals, and the abolition of slavery.

Many of our greatest national leaders—among them Presidents Washington, Jackson, Lincoln, and Wilson—have recognized the influence of the Bible on our country's development. The plainspoken Andrew Jackson referred to the Bible as no less than "the rock on which our Republic rests." Today our beloved America and, indeed, the world, is facing a decade of enormous challenge. As a people we may well be tested as we have seldom, if ever, been tested before. We will need resources of spirit even more than resources of technology, education, and armaments. There could be no more fitting moment than now to reflect with gratitude, humility, and urgency upon the wisdom revealed to us in the writing that Abraham Lincoln called "the best gift God has ever given to man. . . . But for it we could not know right from wrong."

The Congress of the United States, in recognition of the unique contribution of the Bible in shaping the history and character of this nation and so many of its citizens, has by Senate Joint Resolution 165 authorized and requested the president to designate the year 1983 as the "Year of the Bible."

Now, therefore, I Ronald Reagan, President of the United States of America, in recognition of the contributions and influence of the Bible on our Republic and our people, do hereby proclaim 1983 the Year of the Bible in the United States. I encourage all citizens, each in his or her own way, to reexamine and rediscover its priceless and timeless message.

Bill of Rights Day; Human Rights Day and Week
December 9, 1983

Saint John told us, "Ye shall know the truth and the truth shall make you free." Well, in many countries people aren't even allowed to read the Bible. It is up to us to make sure the message of hope and salvation gets through.

You know—I should have brought it with me, although maybe some of you have seen it—but I have a little book, about that big, and about that thick, that contains a verse or two, printed in small type . . . from the Bible. It was smuggled out of Russia and was finally delivered to me as an example of what they do just to try and cling to their faith and belief, that when someone has a Bible, they then take just a verse so that everyone can have at least some words—a few words of the Scripture—something that can be easily hidden. And that, when we think our own freedom, makes it very evident.

National Religious Broadcasters Convention
January 30, 1984

I was pleased last year to proclaim 1983 the Year of the Bible. But, you know, a group called the ACLU severely criticized me for doing that. Well, I wear their indictment like a badge of honor. I believe I stand in pretty good company.

Abraham Lincoln called the Bible "the best gift God has given to man. But for it," he said, "we could not know right from wrong." Like that image of George Washinton kneeling in prayer in the snow at Valley Forge, Lincoln described a people who knew it was not enough to depend on their own courage and goodness; they must also look to God their Father and Preserver. And their faith to walk with him and trust in his Word brought them the blessings of comfort, power, and peace that they sought.

The torch of their faith has been passed from generation to generation. "The grass withereth, the flower fadeth, but the word of our God shall stand forever."

More and more Americans believe that loving God in their hearts is the ultimate value. Last year, not only were Year of the Bible activities held in every state of the union, but more than twenty-five states and 500 cities issued their own Year of the Bible proclamations. One school-

*The Rev. Donn Moomaw, pastor of BelAir
Presbyterian Church, leading in prayer
at Reagan's inauguration. The Reagans
attended BelAir when they lived in
California.*

LORD: for there he offered burnt offerings, and the fat of the peace offerings, because the brasen altar which Sŏl'ŏ-mon had made was not able to receive the burnt offerings, and the meat offerings and the fat.

8 ¶ Also at the same time Sŏl'ŏ-mon kept the feast seven days, and all Ĭs'ra-el with him, a very great congregation, from the entering in of Hā'măth unto the river of E'gypt.

9 And in the eighth day they made a solemn assembly: for they kept the dedication of the altar seven days, and the feast seven days.

10 And on the three and twentieth day of the seventh month he sent the people away into their tents, glad and merry in heart for the goodness that the LORD had shewed unto Dā'vid, and to Sŏl'ŏ-mon, and to Ĭs'ra-el his people.

11 Thus Sŏl'ŏ-mon finished the house of the LORD, and the king's house: and all that came into Sŏl'ŏ-mon's heart to make in the house of the LORD, and in his own house, he prosperously effected.

12 ¶ And the LORD appeared to Sŏl'ŏ-mon by night, and said unto him, I have heard thy prayer, and have chosen this place to myself for an house of sacrifice.

13 If I shut up heaven that there be no rain, or if I command the locusts to devour the land, or if I send pestilence among my people;

14 If my people, which are called by my name, shall humble themselves, and pray, and seek my face, and turn from their wicked ways; then will I hear from heaven, and will forgive their sin, and will heal their land.

15 Now mine eyes shall be open, and mine ears attent unto the prayer *that is made* in this place.

16 For now have I chosen and sanctified this house, that my name may be there for ever: and mine eyes and mine heart shall be there perpetually.

17 And as for thee, if thou wilt walk before me, as Dā'vid thy father walked, and do according to all that I have commanded thee, and shalt observe my statutes and my judgments;

18 Then will I stablish the throne of thy kingdom, according as I have covenanted with Dā'vid thy father, saying, There shall not fail thee a man *to be* ruler in Ĭs'ra-el.

19 But if ye turn away, and forsake my statutes and my commandments, which I have set before you, and shall go and serve other gods, and worship them;

20 Then will I pluck them up by the roots out of my land which I have given them; and this house, which I have sanctified for my name, will I cast out of my sight, and will make it *to be* a proverb and a byword among all nations.

21 And this house, which is high, shall be an astonishment to every one that passeth by it; so that he shall say, Why hath the LORD done thus unto this land, and unto this house?

22 And it shall be answered, Because they forsook the LORD God of their fathers, which brought them forth out of the land of E'gypt,

and laid hold on other gods, and them, and served them: therefo brought all this evil upon them.

CHAPTER 8.

1 *Solomon's buildings.* 7 *The Cananai utaries.* 11 *Pharoah's daughter re house.* 12 *Solomon's yearly solemn He appointeth the priests and Levites* 17 *The navy fetcheth gold from Ophir.*

AND it came to pass at the en years, wherein Sŏl'ŏ-mon ha house of the LORD, and his own h

2 That the cities which Hū'răm to Sŏl'ŏ-mon, Sŏl'ŏ-mon built caused the children of Ĭs'ra-el to d

3 And Sŏl'ŏ-mon went to Hā'ma and prevailed against it.

4 And he built Tăd'mŏr in the and all the store cities, which Hā'măth.

5 Also he built Bĕth-hŏr'ŏn the Bĕth-hŏr'ŏn the nether, fenced walls, gates, and bars;

6 And Bā'ā-lăth, and all the that Sŏl'ŏ-mon had, and all the ch and the cities of the horsemen, a Sŏl'ŏ-mon desired to build in J and in Lĕb'a-non, and througho land of his dominion.

7 ¶ *As for* all the people *that wer* Hĭt'tites, and the Am'ō-rites, and zites, and the Hī'vites, and the which *were* not of Ĭs'ra-el.

8 *But* of their children, who we them in the land, whom the childre consumed not, them did Sŏl'ŏ-mc pay tribute until this day.

9 But of the children of Ĭs'ra-el di make no servants for his work: bu men of war, and chief of his ca captains of his chariots and horse

10 And these *were* the chief of mon's officers, *even* two hundred that bare rule over the people.

11 ¶ And Sŏl'ŏ-mon brought up th of Phăr'aŏh out of the city of D the house that he had built for said, My wife shall not dwell in of Dā'vid king of Ĭs'ra-el, because *are* holy, whereunto the ark of the come.

12 ¶ Then Sŏl'ŏ-mon offered buru unto the LORD on the altar o which he had built before the porc

13 Even after a certain rate offering according to the comma Mō'ses, on the sabbaths, and on moons, and on the solemn feasts, in the year, *even* in the feast of bread, and in the feast of weeks, feast of tabernacles.

14 ¶ And he appointed, accordi order of Dā'vid his father, the cou priests to their service, and the their charges, to praise and mini the priests, as the duty of every da the porters also by their courses gate: for so had Dā'vid the man o manded.

15 And they departed not from

Nelle Reagan's Bible open to one of President Reagan's favorite verses. It was open to this page when he was sworn in to office.

king unto the priests and
g any matter, or concern-

ork of Sŏl'ŏ-mon was pre-
y of the foundation of
, and until it was finished.
ie LORD was perfected.
Sŏl'ŏ-mon to E'zĭ-ŏn-gē'bĕr,
the sea side in the land of

sent him by the hands of
s, and servants that had
sea; and they went with
Sŏl'ŏ-mon to O'phĭr, and
hundred and fifty talents
ght *them* to king Sŏl'ŏ-mon.

HAPTER 9.
admireth the wisdom of Solomon.
17 *His throne of ivory.* 20 *His*
ceeding riches and wisdom. 31

queen of She'bă heard of
l'ŏ-mon, she came to prove
rd questions at Jĕ-rŭ'să-lĕm,
company, and camels that
old in abundance, and pre-
when she was come to Sŏl'-
uned with him of all that

told her all her questions:
othing hid from Sŏl'ŏ-mon
r not.
queen of She'bă had seen
'ŏ-mon, and the house that

of his table, and the sitting
and the attendance of his
eir apparel; his cupbearers
apparel; and his ascent by
up into the house of the
no more spirit in her.
to the king, *It was a* true
eard in mine own land of
f thy wisdom:
eved not their words, until
eyes had seen *it:* and behold
ne greatness of thy wisdom
for thou exceedest the fame

men, and happy *are* these
ich stand continually before
r wisdom.
ne LORD thy God, which
to set thee on his throne,
LORD thy God: because thy
l, to establish them for ever,
ae thee king over them, to
justice.
the king an hundred and
d gold, and of spices great
precious stones: neither
uch spice as the queen of
g Sŏl'ŏ-mon.
vants also of Hū'răm, and
Sŏl'ŏ-mon, which brought
r, brought ăl'gŭm trees and

g made *of* the ăl'gŭm trees
ouse of the LORD, and to the
d harps and psalteries for

singers: and there were none such seen before
in the land of Jū'dăh.

12 And king Sŏl'ŏ-mon gave to the queen of
She'bă all her desire, whatsoever she asked,
beside *that* which she had brought unto the
king. So she turned and went away to her
own land, she and her servants.

13 ¶ Now the weight of gold that came to
Sŏl'ŏ-mon in one year was six hundred and
threescore and six talents of gold;

14 Beside *that which* chapmen and merchants
brought. And all the kings of A-rā'bĭ-ă
and governors of the country brought gold
and silver to Sŏl'ŏ-mon.

15 ¶ And king Sŏl'ŏ-mon made two hundred
targets *of* beaten gold; six hundred *shĕ'kĕls*
of beaten gold went to one target.

16 And three hundred shields *made he of*
beaten gold; three hundred she'kĕls of gold
went to one shield. And the king put them
in the house of the forest of Lĕb'ă-non.

17 Moreover the king made a great throne
of ivory, and overlaid it with pure gold.

18 And *there were* six steps to the throne,
with a footstool of gold, *which were* fastened
to the throne, and stays on each side of the
sitting place, and two lions standing by the
stays:

19 And twelve lions stood there on the
one side and on the other upon the six steps.
There was not the like made in any kingdom.

20 ¶ And all the drinking vessels of king Sŏl'-
ŏ-mon *were of* gold, and all the vessels of the
house of the forest of Lĕb'ă-non *were of* pure
gold: none *were of* silver; it was *not* anything
accounted of in the days of Sŏl'ŏ-mon.

21 For the king's ships went to Tar'shĭsh
with the servants of Hū'răm: every three
years once came the ships of Tar'shĭsh bringing gold, and silver, ivory, and apes, and
peacocks.

22 And king Sŏl'ŏ-mon passed all the kings
of the earth in riches and wisdom.

23 ¶ And all the kings of the earth sought
the presence of Sŏl'ŏ-mon, to hear his wisdom,
that God had put in his heart.

24 And they brought every man his present,
vessels of silver, and vessels of gold, and
raiment, harness, and spices, horses, and
mules, a rate year by year.

25 ¶ And Sŏl'ŏ-mon had four thousand
stalls for horses and chariots, and twelve
thousand horsemen; whom he bestowed in
the chariot cities, and with the king at Jĕ-
rŭ'să-lĕm.

26 And he reigned over all the kings from
the river even unto the land of the Phĭl'ĭs-
tines, and to the border of E'gypt.

27 And the king made silver in Jĕ-rŭ'să-lĕm
as stones, and cedar trees made he as the
sycomore trees that *are* in the low plains in
abundance.

28 And they brought unto Sŏl'ŏ-mon horses
out of E'gypt, and out of all lands.

29 ¶ Now the rest of the acts of Sŏl'ŏ-mon,
first and last, *are* they not written in the
book of Nā'thăn the prophet, and in the
prophecy of A-hī'jăh the Shī'lō-nite, and in the
visions of Ĭd'dō the seer against Jĕr-ŏ-bō'ăm
the son of Nē'băt?

Reagan working on an upcoming address.

*The President visits with children in a
Washington-area public school.*

The President in prayer at the National Association of Evangelicals' 42nd annual convention.

Reagan declaring 1983 the Year of the Bible.

President Reagan meeting with Moral Majority leader, the Rev. Jerry Falwell.

The President with Rabbi Shlomo Goren.

Reagan with Pope John Paul II at the Vatican.

The Reagans receiving Mother Teresa at the White House.

*Some lighthearted teasing shared between
the President and First Lady in the Oval Office.*

teacher, Mary Gibson, in New York, raised $4,000 to buy Bibles for working people in downtown Manhattan.

Nineteen eighty-three was the year more of us read the Good Book. Can we make a resolution here today? That 1984 will be the year we put its great truths into action?

My experience in this office I hold has only deepened a belief I've held for many years: Within the covers of that single Book are all the answers to all the problems that face us today—if we'd only read and believe.

SEVEN

VANGUARDS OF AMERICA'S FUTURE

The President's Statements on Family and the Sanctity of Life

When I think of the wisdom and scope of his plan I fall down on my knees and pray to the Father of all the great family of God—some of them already in heaven and some down here on earth (Ephesians 3:14,15, TLB).

Mother's Day Proclamation
April 13, 1981

Each year our nation designates Mother's Day as a moment of special tribute and appreciation for the mothers of America.

Recent years have brought many changes to the lives of Ameican mothers. Today they are increasingly involved in business, politics, education, arts, sciences, and government as well as the vital work of the home and family. Yet, whether they seek careers outside the home or work as homemakers, they remain the heart of the American family.

They shape the character of our people through the love and nurture of their children. It is the strength they give their families that keeps our nation strong.

On this Mother's Day, we express our deep personal gratitude to our own mothers and thank all those women whose devotion to their families helps sustain a healthy and productive citizenry.

Now, therefore, I, Ronald Reagan, President of the

United States of America, do hereby designate Sunday, May 10, 1981, as Mother's Day. I direct government officials to display the flag of the United States on all federal government buildings, and I urge all citizens to display the flag at their homes and other suitable places on that day.

Father's Day Proclamation
May 20, 1981

There is no institution more vital to our nation's survival than the American family. Here the seeds of personal character are planted, the roots of public virtue first nourished. Through love and instruction, discipline, guidance and example, we learn from our mothers and fathers the values that will shape our private lives and our public citizenship.

The days of our childhood forecast our lives, as poets and philosophers long have told us. "The childhood shows the man as morning shows the day," John Milton wrote. "Train up a child in the way he should go: and when he is old, he will not depart from it," Solomon tells us. Clearly, the future is in the care of our parents. Such is the responsibility, promise, and hope of fatherhood. Such is the gift that our fathers give us.

Our fathers bear an awesome responsibility—one that they shoulder willingly and fulfill with a love that asks no recompense. By turns both gentle and firm, our fathers guide us along the path from infancy to adulthood. We embody their joy, pain, and sacrifice, and inherit memories more cherished than any possession.

On Father's Day each year, we express formally a love and gratitude whose roots go deeper than conscious memory can recite. It is only fitting that we have this special day to pay tribute to those men—who deserve our deepest respect and devotion. It is equally fitting, as we recall the ancient and loving command to honor our fathers, that we resolve to do so by becoming ourselves parents and citizens who are worthy of honor.

Now, therefore, I, Ronald Reagan, President of the United States of America, do hereby proclaim, in accordance with the Joint Resolution of Congress, that Sunday, June 21, 1981, be observed as Father's Day. I call upon all citizens to mark this day with appropriate public and private expressions of the honor we owe our fathers, and invite the states and local communities throughout the nation to observe Father's Day with appropriate ceremonies.

President's News Conference
January 19, 1982

Question: Mr. President, as you know, this Congress has attached the most restrictive anti-abortion language to the Health and Human Services money bill. It would ban all abortion for low-income women except if the mother's life would be endangered by completing the pregnancy, and it would make no exceptions for rape or incest. My question to you is—and I would like to have a follow-up—if one of your daughters were unfortunate enough to be raped and become pregnant as a result, would you agree with this law that she should be forced to carry that pregnancy to term?

The President: I have been one who believes that abortion is the taking of a human life. And I know the difficulty of the question that you ask. I also do know that—because I won't answer it in that personal term—but I do know that I once approved the law in California [allowing] that as a justification in the line of self-defense, just as a mother has a right, in my view, to protect her own life at the expense of the life of the unborn child. I am very concerned, because I have found out since, that that was used as a gigantic loophole in the law, and . . . it literally led to abortion on demand on the plea of rape.

Now, I wish I could have a solid answer for you. On that basis, I would be hesitant to approve abortion.

Question: May I ask you something on a related point, sir? There is pending in the Senate a constitutional amendment sponsored by Senator Hatch that would permit Congress and any state to ban abortions for all women, rich or poor. When Senator Hatch opened his hearings on that he said that his religion prompted him to support that amendment, and at the same time, as you know, there are many other religious faiths who consider it an invasion of privacy.

Also, in view of that divisiveness and in view of the fact that the public opinion polls show that most Americans favor freedom of choice on abortion, have you given this any second thought or rethought your position at all?

The President: I can't say that I have really looked at or studied this particular proposal. I can just say to you that following up on the hearings that were held on the Hill as to when life begins, I think that everyone has overlooked the real finding. The fact that they could not resolve the issue of when life begins was a finding in and of itself. If we don't know, then shouldn't we morally opt on the side that it is life?

If you came upon an immobile body and you yourself could not determine whether it was dead or alive, I think that you would decide to consider it alive until somebody could prove it was dead. You wouldn't get a shovel and start covering it up. And I think we should do the same thing with regard to abortion.

National Religious Broadcasters Convention
February 9, 1982

To preserve our blessed land, we must look to God. And we must look to the hearthstone, because that's where all hope for America lies. Families are the bedrock of our nation—teachers of cooperation, tolerance, concern, and responsibility. Rebuilding America begins with restoring family strength and preserving family values.

Conservative Political Action Conference
February 26, 1982

We must with calmness and resolve help the vast majority of our fellow Americans understand that the more than one and one-half million abortions performed in America in 1980 amount to a great moral evil, an assault on the sacredness of human life.

National Right to Life Convention
July 1982

Last year there were more than one and one-half million abortions in America. This is an assault on the sacredness of human life.

No one in America is more sensitive to this enormous tragedy and no one in America has done more to put a stop to it than those of you attending this right-to-life convention. It is you who have attempted to protect the helpless and speak for the unborn; you have carried the burden and fought the good fight. For this, God will bless you; and for this, millions of Americans, myself included, thank you.

But now—as Congress approaches the three-quarter mark in its current session—you deserve much more than thanks or mere verbal support. And certainly the hundreds of thousands, and perhaps millions, of unborn children who face extinction this year deserve much more than words— they deserve to have their right to life fully protected by law. The time has come for Congress to face the national tragedy of abortion, to fully discuss and debate on the House and Senate floors the heartbreaking dimensions of this tragedy.

Those of you who supported pro-life candidates in the 1980 election—and those of us who as candidates actively spoke out against abortion—cannot be accused of being irresponsible or overly zealous in our pursuit of human life legislation. We have been patient and realistic. Last year we understood that past national policies had headed our country well down the road to economic disaster. We knew we had to deal with this momentous problem; we did so with urgency and effectiveness. I know that many of you supported and worked hard for this Administration's Program for Economic Recovery.

But as I said a few months after taking office . . . this Administration does not and will not have separate agendas—one for economic matters, one for the so-called "social" issues. Our concern is to make America healthy: economically, morally, in every way. Abortion is an inescapable national dilemma. It is a problem that cannot wait; it must be confronted.

The abortion tragedy is after all one of the greatest moral—and potentially one of the most divisive—issues to ever face this country. As history shows in the case of other such great issues, attempting to ignore them only causes a deeper disarray in our national life and increases the potential for disunity and disruption.

The Supreme Court's ruling that legalized abortion will continue to have a profound and painful impact on our nation until it is properly addressed by the people through their elected representatives. Only the other day, a federal judge in Connecticut reopened the whole legal debate on this matter when he ruled that a fetus had civil rights, including the right to sue an alleged attacker. Recently, a report by the Senate Judiciary Committee emphasized the far-reaching impact of the abortion tragedy by concluding that the effect of the U.S. Supreme Court decisions has been to legalize abortion right up until the moment of birth.

A few months ago, in my own state of California, a garage was discovered containing the bodies of 17,000 abortion victims—many of them late-term. The pictures I have seen are heartrending and clearly show abortion is an assault on human life.

And only a few months ago, many of us read of a child in Bloomington, Indiana, permitted by the courts to die only because he was handicapped.

As George Will would write in an emotional but carefully reasoned—and, I might add, unforgettable—essay, the freedom to do away with inconvenient life is now being extended—just as those of us who are part of the right to life movement predicted—beyond fetal life to entirely new categories of life.

That is why the House and Senate must deal with the abortion issue. Major human life measures, such as Senator Helms' Human Life Bill, Senator Hatch's Human Life Federalism Amendment and Senator Hatfield's Abortion Funding Restriction Bill, deserve full consideration by the Senate this session. Believe me, in all of this, I share your sense of urgency.

You know, it has always puzzled me that those who favor abortion will argue that because a child is not old enough or wanted enough that it is an act of kindness to deny him or her the chance of life.

C. S. Lewis once wrote that "love is something more stern and splendid than mere kindness." This is a critical insight into the present debate over abortion and it is something of what I meant when I wrote to George Will about his column on that child in Bloomington—a column in which George mentioned his own handicapped son, Jonathan.

"Jonathan is indeed fortunate," I wrote, "that God has chosen the Wills for his parents; and, as I see from your column, the Wills are even more fortunate that God has given them Jonathan."

This is the heart of the matter. The world is not ours to superintend—nor is innocent life ours to dispense with or terminate. Those decisions belong to another—another to whom suffering in our world is fully comprehensible and who counts our resignation in these matters to our credit. It is his guidance we seek now and in all of our future efforts.

Obviously, the days ahead will be important ones in the struggle for human life legislation. And what you do during the next few days will be vital to the success of our efforts in this great cause. I want you to know that you have my wholehearted support and my fervent prayers for your success.

Constitutional Amendment for a Balanced Federal Budget
July 19, 1982

Families stand at the center of society. They are the vanguards of America's future. Yet, how can families and family values flourish when big government, with its power to tax, inflate, and regulate, has absorbed their wealth, usurped their rights, and too often crushed their spirit?

Knights of Columbus Address, Hartford, Connecticut
August 3, 1982

I also strongly believe, as you have been told, that the protection of innocent life is and has always been a legitmate, indeed, the first duty of government. And, believing that, I favor human life. And I believe in the human life legislation. The Senate now has three proposals on this matter from Senators Hatch, Helms, and Hatfield. The national tragedy of abortion on demand must end. I'm urging the Senate to give these proposals the speedy consideration they deserve.

Anti-Abortion Amendment to Federal Debt Ceiling Legislation
September 8, 1982

A broad spectrum of concerned Americans are joining with me in calling upon the Senate to bring to an end its debate on Senator Helms' anti-abortion amendment to the debt ceiling bill. Senator Hatch, whose Constitutional Abortion Amendment I continue to support, has generously joined in the call for a vote on the amendment now before the Senate.

This amendment is a responsible statutory approach to one of the most sensitive problems our society faces— the taking of the life of an unborn child. Specifically, the Senate is debating an amendment which:

    1. Affirms the humanity of the unborn child in our society.

2. Bans permanently federal funding and support for the taking of the life of an unborn child except to save the life of the mother.
3. Provides opportunity for the Supreme Court to reconsider its usurpation of the role of legislatures and state courts in this area.

I realize that this amendment reflects a moderate approach. My purpose is not to impede any other anti-abortion measures, including Senator Hatch's amendment, that may come before you. But this is the first clear-cut vote in this Congress on the humanity of the unborn, and it is crucial that a filibuster not prevent the representatives of our citizens from expressing their judgment on so vital a matter.

It is time to stand and be counted on this issue. I urge you to lend your support to Senator Baker's petition to invoke cloture on this measure.

Beyond the matter of cloture, it is vitaly important for the Congress to affirm, as this amendment does, the fundamental principle that all human life has intrinsic value. We must never become a society in which an individual has the right to do away with inconvenient life. I ask that you keep these thoughts in mind when you vote your conscience on the amendment.

Alfred M. Landon Lecture Series on Public Issues
September 9, 1982

I know now what I'm about to say will be very controversial, but I also believe that God's greatest gift is human life and that we have a sacred duty to protect the innocent human life of an unborn child. Now I realize that this view is not shared by all. But out of all the debate on this subject has come one undisputed fact, and this, out of the debate, has been the uncertainty of when life begins. And I just happen to believe that simple morality dictates that unless and until someone can prove the unborn human is not alive, we must give it the benefit of the doubt and assume it is. And thus, it should be entitled to life, liberty, and the pursuit of happiness.

The White House, Washington, D.C.
January 21, 1983

Nancy and I are very pleased to extend our warmest greetings and best wishes to all those gathered from across the land for this historic "March for Life."

This nation was founded by men and women who shared a strong moral vision of the great value of each and every individual. America has come to symbolize that belief for the rest of the world. But the tragic United States Supreme Court decision which legalized "abortion on demand" in 1973 severely tests our moral commitments.

You are assembled here to commemorate the tenth anniversary of the Roe v. Wade decision and to march and pray for its reversal. We join you in that hope and plea. The abortion decision was a tragedy, and we have the responsibility to do all we can to protect unborn children.

As one who not only shares your anguish over the taking of an unborn child's life but is committed to the sanctity of all innocent human life, I applaud your demonstrated humanitarian concern and leadership in this vital issue.

We have waited ten years for Congress to rectify the tragedy of Roe v. Wade. The time for action is now. I assure you that in the ninety-eighth Congress I will support any appropriate legislative action that will restrict abortion.

I am especially pleased to see that a Respect Human Life Act has already been introduced in this Congess by Representative Henry Hyde. Not only does this bill strengthen and expand restrictions on abortion, but it also addresses the problem of infanticide by making clear the right of all children, including those who are handicapped, to appropriate medical treatment.

May this march prove a hallmark in the struggle to correct a great wrong, and may God bless your efforts in the future.

Radio Address to the Nation
January 22, 1983

There's another issue closely identified with families, although the issue itself often splits families apart. Ten years ago today, the Supreme Court overturned the state laws protecting the lives of the unborn. Heated debate on abortion has raged ever since. On one hand, there is the argument that a woman should have control over her own person. On the other hand, there is the argument that another life is involved here—the unborn child. That's the belief which has drawn many here to Washington today to march and to pray.

I, too, have always believed that God's greatest gift is human life and that we have a duty to protect the life of an unborn child. Until someone can prove the unborn child is not a life, shouldn't we give it the benefit of the doubt and assume it is? That's why I favored legislation to end the practice of abortion on demand and why I will continue to support it in the new Congress.

Now, some of you may be thinking, "Well, he hasn't said a thing that's new." I guess that's true. Some values shouldn't change. But I want you to know there are certain family issues I'll advocate even though it's the budget and the economy that will be getting the headlines, expecially in the days ahead.

National Religious Broadcasters Convention
January 31, 1983

There's another struggle we must wage to redress a great national wrong. We must go forward with unity of purpose and will. And let us come together, Christians and Jews, let us pray together, march, lobby, and mobilize every force we have, so that we can end the tragic taking of unborn children's lives. Who among us can imagine the excruciating pain the unborn must feel as their lives are snuffed away? And we know medically they do feel pain.

I'm glad that a Respect Human Life Act has already been introduced in Congress by Representative Henry Hyde. Not only does this bill strengthen and expand restrictions on abortions financed by tax dollars, it also addresses the problem of infanticide. It makes clear the right of all children, including those who are born handicapped, to food and appropriate medical treatment after birth, and it has the full support of this administration.

I know that many well-intentioned, sincerely motivated people believe that government intervention violates a woman's right of choice. And they would be right if there were any proof that the unborn are not living human beings. Medical evidence indicates to the contrary and, if that were not enough, how do we explain the survival of babies who are born prematurely, some very prematurely?

We once believed that the heart didn't start beating until the fifth month. But as medical instrumentation has improved, we've learned the heart [starts] beating long before that. Doesn't the constitutional protection of life, liberty, and the pursuit of happiness extend to the unborn unless it can be proven beyond a shadow of a doubt that life does not exist in the unborn? And I believe the burden of proof is on those who would make that point.

I read in the Washington Post about a young woman named Victoria. She's with child, and she said, "In this society we save whales, we save timber wolves and bald eagles and Coke bottles. Yet everyone wanted me to throw away my baby." Well, Victoria's story has a happy ending. Her baby will be born.

Victoria has received assistance from a Christian couple, and from Sav-A-Life, a new Dallas group run by Jim McKee, a concerned citizen who thinks it's important to provide constructive alternatives to abortion. There's hope for America. She remains powerful and a powerful force for good, and it's thanks to the conviction and commitment of people like those who are helping Victoria. They're living the meaning of the two great commandments: "Thou shalt love the Lord thy God with all thy heart, and with all thy soul, and with all thy might" and "Thou shalt love thy neighbour as thyself."

Question and Answer Session
February 1983

Question: Mr. President, I am a worker in the pro-life, anti-abortion movement. I can assure you that many citizens voted for you in the last election only because of your pro-life position. Can we now count on you to use your tremendous powers of persuasion to unite our pro-life members of Congress behind legislation that will stop the killing of the unborn?

The President: Yesterday afternoon I spoke to an audience of this same size, 4,000 people, in Washington, and pledged to them that I am going to continue to do everything I can.

I realize that there are people who sincerely and honestly believe that it is an unwarranted intrusion into the privacy and the right of choice of women who may choose to go that way. But I have to feel that until and unless someone can prove beyond shadow of a doubt that the unborn child is not a living human being, then we have to opt in favor that it is alive. It is killing to do what is being done today. And that we only condone in self-defense.

National Association of Evangelicals Convention
March 8, 1983

More than a decade ago, a Supreme Court decision literally wiped off the books of fifty states statutes protecting the rights of unborn children. Abortion on demand now takes the lives of up to one and one-half million unborn children a year. Human life legislation ending this tragedy will some day pass the Congress, and you and I must never rest until it does. Unless and until it can be proven that the unborn child is not a living entity, then its right to life, liberty, and the pursuit of happiness must be protected.

You may remember that when abortion on demand began, many, and indeed, I'm sure many of you, warned that the practice would lead to a decline in respect for human life, that the philosophical premises used to justify abortion on demand would ultimately be used to justify other attacks on the sacredness of human life—infanticide or mercy killing. Tragically enough, those warnings proved all too true. Only last year a court permitted the death by starvation of a handicapped infant.

I have directed the Health and Human Services Department to make clear to every health care facility in the United States that the Rehabilitation Act of 1973 protects all handicapped persons against discrimination based on handicaps, including infants. And we have taken the further step of requiring that each and every recipient of federal funds who provides health care services to infants must post and keep posted in a conspicuous place a notice stating that "discriminatory failure to feed and care for handicapped infants in this facility is prohibited by federal law." It also lists a twenty-four-hour, toll-free number so that nurses and others may report violations in time to save the infant's life.

Radio Address to the Nation
May 7, 1983

This is a very special weekend in American life, a time specially set aside to honor our mothers and the mothers of our children. As we do, we acknowledge their role as the heart of our families and reinforce our families as the cornerstone of our society.

In our families, and often from our mothers, we first learn about values and caring and the difference between right and wrong. Those of us blessed with loving families draw our confidence from them and the strength we need to face the world. We also first learn at home, and, again, often from our mothers, about the God who will guide us through life.

The mothers we honor this weekend, young or not so young, partners or alone, well-to-do or sometimes agonizingly poor, are as diverse as our varied population. But they share a commitment to future generations and a yearning to improve the world their children will inherit. They shape the America we know today and are now molding the character of our country tomorrow.

Since men seem to have written most of our history books, the role of women and mothers in our communities and families has not always been given its due. But the truth is the wild west could never have been tamed, the vast prairies never plowed, nor God and learning brought to the corners of our continent without the strength, bravery, and influence of our grandmothers, great-grandmothers, and the women who came before them.

Living through blizzards, plagues, prairie fires, and floods, these women made homes and started families, organized churches, and built schools. They served as teachers, field hands, physicians, and the center of the family.

I was reading a book recently about Kansas frontier women and came across a passage that seemed to sum it all up. Esther Clark wrote, "Mother has always been the gamest one of us. I can remember her hanging onto the reins of a runaway mule team, her black hair tumbling out of its pins and over her shoulders, her face set and white while one small girl clung with chattering teeth to the sides of the rocking wagon and a baby sister bounced about on the floor in paralyzed wonder.

"I remember, too, the things the men said about Leny's nerve. But I think as much courage as it took to hang onto the reins that day, it took more to live twenty-four hours at a time, month in and out on the lonely and lovely prairie without giving up to the loneliness."

Of course, Leny's nerve and strength are echoed in modern-day women and mothers who face different but equally trying tests of their courage. There are mothers like Rachel Rossow of Connecticut, for example, and Dorothy DeBolt of California, who with their husbands have adopted between them twenty-five handicapped boys and girls in addition to their own children.

I had a chance to visit with Rachel and her family last month, and I can tell you I've never seen a happier group. I know the strains on them must be great, emotionally and financially, but not as great as the love they feel for each other.

Of course, many millions of American mothers are quiet, everyday heroes struggling to stretch budgets and too often maintaining their families alone. Many also contribute to society through full-time careers, and others are forced to work just to make ends meet. They're raising children in a fast-paced world where basic values are constantly questioned. Their monumental challenge is to bring their children into adulthood, healthy and whole, nurturing their physical and emotional growth while avoiding the pitfalls of drug abuse and crime.

The lives of American mothers today are far removed from the prairies, and yet they have a nobility about them, too. Government should help, not hinder parents in this task. And that's why our policies have been designed to restore the family to its rightful place in our society, combat the inflation that stole from family budgets, expand opportunity through a renewed economy and hasten the return of values and principles that made America both great and good.

On the economic front, I think we've made some solid progress in bringing relief to your financially strapped families. When we took office, inflation was at 12.4 percent, but it's only been one-half of one percent for the last six months. You can see a difference on the grocery shelves. A loaf of bread, for example, costs only two cents more now than it did in 1980. If we'd continued with the old rate of inflation, by now it would have cost eleven cents more. Milk is about sixteen cents cheaper than it would have been, hamburger about eighteen cents cheaper per pound, and the savings on a dozen eggs is as much as fifty cents. I don't have to tell the people who do the shopping how these savings add up. But for those of you who don't, we estimate that a family of four on a fixed income of $20,000 has $1,700 more in purchasing power this year than they would have had under the old inflation rate.

The progress we're making with the economy, just like the national renewal we're seeing spring up all around us, is the product of our reliance again on good old-fashioned common sense, renewed belief in ourselves, and faith in God.

Now and then I find guidance and direction in the worn brown Bible I used to take the oath of office. It's been the Reagan family Bible, and, like many of yours, has its flyleaf filled with important events; its margins are scrawled with insights and passages underlined for emphasis. My mother, Nelle, made all those marks in that book. She used it to instruct her two young sons, and I look to it still.

A passage in Proverbs describes the ideal woman, saying: "Strength and dignity are her clothing, and she smiles at the future. She opens her mouth in wisdom, and the teaching of kindness is on her tongue. Give her the product of her hands, and let her works praise her in the gates."

Well, that passage calls for us to recognize the enormous strengths and contributions of women, wives, and mothers and indicates to me that society always needs a little reminding. Well, let us use this weekend as a symbol that we will always remember, reward, and recognize them and use their examples of love and courage as inspiration to be better than we are.

Father's Day Proclamation
June 1, 1983

Each year this nation sets aside a day on which to honor fathers for their many contributions to the well-being of their children, their families, and our society.

Traditionally, Americans have looked to fathers to provide leadership and stability for their families. Fathers play a vital role in providing sustenance, protection, and guidance for their families and the community at large. We owe them our high esteem, for their presence and gift of love as role models, providers, and defenders of the nation. They not only play an invaluable part in transmitting the values and traditions of our society, but are instrumental in encouraging the self-confidence of our youngsters in facing the future.

Fatherhood is both a great responsibility and one of the most rewarding and pleasurable experiences life has to offer. Father's Day presents a special opportunity to appreciate our fathers—to consider all they have done, and all they continue to do, in fostering children's physical and emotional growth, encouraging success, easing failure, maintaining family life, contributing vitally to the economy, and serving their communities. The quality and scope of their families and our country inspire and strengthen us as individuals and as a nation.

Supreme Court Decision on Abortion Laws
June 16, 1983

Our society is confronted with a great moral issue—taking of the life of an unborn child. Accordingly, I join millions of Americans expressing profound disappointment at the decisions announced by the Supreme Court in striking down several efforts by states and localities to control the circumstances under which abortion may be performed.

As Justice O'Connor emphasized in her dissenting opinion joined by Justices White and Rehnquist, the legislature is the appropriate forum for resolving these issues. The issue of abortion must be resolved by our democratic process.

Once again I call on the Congress to make its voice heard against abortion on demand and to restore legal protections for the unborn whether by statute or constitutional amendment.

National Family Week Proclamation
November 4, 1983

The family and family life are central to our American heritage. Family bonds give us an anchor in the past, as well as hope for the future. It is within the family that tradition is created, individuals grow, and faith is nurtured. Through family living, we discover who we are, how to interact with our fellow man, and the values that make a free society possible.

Families perform the daily tasks that sustain and renew us, including raising children and caring for the elderly. Families not only provide better health but also serve the special needs of the handicapped. In particular, those who have opened their homes through adoption and foster care deserve special thanks for offering the gift of family life to our nation's less fortunate children.

Today, amid new pressures and needs, America is relearning the importance of its families. For instance, success in the national fight against drug and alcohol abuse must begin with a strong and united family. We are newly aware that the family cannot be taken for granted, and that the support of a family can never truly be replicated.

In recognition of the importance of the family as an essential unit of our free and orderly society, the Congress, by Senate Joint Resolution 45, has authorized and requested the President to designate the week beginning on November 20, 1983, as "National Family Week."

Now, therefore, I, Ronald Reagan, President of the United States of America, do hereby proclaim the week of November 20 through November 26, 1983, as National Family Week. I applaud the men and women who uphold our families in many ways, as parents, grandparents, as the daughters and sons of older Americans.

I invite the governors of the several states, the chief officials of local governments and all our citizens to observe Thanksgiving Day, I especially invite all Americans to give thanks for the family relationships with which we have been blessed.

Radio Address to the Nation
December 3, 1983

This is a very special time of year for us, a time for family reunions and for celebrating together the blessings of God and the promises he has given us. From Thanksgiving to Hanukkah, which our Jewish community is now celebrating, to Christmas in three weeks' time, this is a season of hope and of love.

Certainly one of the greatest blessings for people everywhere is the family itself. The American Family Institute recently dedicated its book of essays, *The Family in the Modern World,* to Maria Victoria Walesa, daughter of Danuta and Lech Walesa, to whose christening came 7,000 Poles expressing their belief that the family remains the foundation of freedom. And, of course, they're right. It's in the family where we learn to think for ourselves, care for others, and acquire the values of self-reliance, integrity, responsibility, and compassion.

Families stand at the center of society, so building our future must begin by preserving family values. Tragically, too many in Washington have been asking us to swallow a whopper: namely, that bigger government is the greatest force for fairness and progress. But this so-called solution has given most of us a bad case of financial indigestion. How can families survive when big government's powers to tax, inflate, and regulate absorb their wealth, usurp their rights, and crush their spirit? Was there compassion for a working family in 21.5 percent interest rates, 12.5 percent inflation, and taxes soaring out of sight? Consider the cost of child-rearing. It now takes $85,000 to raise a child to age eighteen, and family incomes haven't kept up. During the 1970s real wages actually declined over 2 percent. Consider taxes. In 1948 the tax on the average two-child family was just nine dollars. Today it is $2,900.

As economic and social pressures have increased, the bonds that bind families together have come under strain. For example, three times as many families are headed by single parents today as in 1960. Many single parents make heroic sacrifices and deserve all our support. But there is no question that many well-intentioned Great Society-type programs contributed to family breakups, welfare dependency, and a large increase in births out of wedlock. In the 1970s the number of single mothers rose from 8 to 13 percent among whites and from 31 to a tragic 47 percent among blacks. Too often their children grow up poor, malnourished, and lacking in motivation. It's a path to social and health problems, low school performance, unemployment, and delinquency.

If we strengthen families, we'll help reduce poverty and the whole range of other social problems.

We can begin by reducing the economic burdens of inflation and taxes, and we're doing this. Since 1980 inflation has been chopped by three-fourths. Taxes have been cut for every family that earns a living, and we've increased the tax credit for child care. Yesterday we learned that our growing economy reduced unemployment to 8.2 percent last month. The payroll employment figure went up by 370,000 jobs.

At the same time, new policies are helping our neediest families move from dependence to independence. Our new job training law will train over a million needy and unemployed Americans each year for productive jobs. I should add that our enterprise zones proposal would stimulate new businesses, bringing jobs and hope to some of the most destitute areas of the country. The Senate has adopted this proposal. But after two years of delay, the House Democratic leadership only recently agreed to hold its first hearing on the legislation. This is a jobs bill America needs. And come January, we expect action.

We've made prevention of drug abuse among youth a top priority. We'll soon announce a national missing-children's center to help find and rescue children who've been abducted and exploited. We're working with states and local communities to increase the adoption of special-needs children. More children with permanent homes mean fewer children with permanent problems.

We're also stiffening the enforcement of child support from absent parents. And we're trying hard to improve education through more discipline, a return to the basics, and through reforms like tuition tax credits to help hard-working parents.

In coming months, we'll propose new ways to help families stay together, remain independent, and cope with the pressures of modern life. A cornerstone of our efforts must be assisting families to support themselves. As Franklin Roosevelt said almost fifty years ago, "Self-help and self-control are the essence of the American tradition."

In Washington everyone looks out for special interest groups. Well, I think families are pretty special. And with your help, we'll continue looking out for their interests.

National Sanctity of Human Life Day
January 13, 1984

The values and freedoms we cherish as Americans rest on our fundamental commitment to the sanctity of human life. The first of the "unalienable rights" affirmed by our Declaration of Independence is the right to life itself, a right [that] the Declaration states has been endowed by our Creator on all human beings—whether young or old, weak or strong, healthy or handicapped.

Since 1973, however, more than 15 million unborn children have died in legalized abortions—a tragedy of stunning dimensions that stands in sad contrast to our belief that each life is sacred. These children, over tenfold the number of Americans lost in all our nation's wars, will never laugh, never sing, never experience the joy of human love; nor will they strive to heal the sick, or feed the poor, or make peace among nations. Abortion has denied them the first and most basic of human rights, and we are infinitely poorer for their loss.

We are poorer not simply for lives not led and for contributions not made, but also for the erosion of our sense of the worth and dignity of every individual. To diminish the value of one category of human life is to diminish us all. Slavery, which treated blacks as something less than human, to be bought and sold if convenient, cheapened human life and mocked our dedication to the freedom and equality of all men and women. Can we say that abortion—which treats the unborn as something less than human, to be destroyed if convenient—will be less corrosive to the values we hold dear?

We have been given the precious gift of human life, made more precious still by our births in or pilgrimages to a land of freedom. It is fitting, then, on the anniversary of the Supreme Court decision in Roe v. Wade that struck

117

down state anti-abortion laws, that we reflect anew on these blessings, and on our corresponding responsibility to guard with care the lives and freedoms of even the weakest of our fellow human beings.

Now, therefore, I Ronald Reagan, President of the United States of America, do hereby proclaim Sunday, January 22, 1984, as National Sanctity of Human Life Day. I call upon the citizens of this blessed land to gather on that day in homes and places of worship to give thanks for the gift of life, and to reaffirm our commitment to the dignity of every human being and the sanctity of each human life.

The State of the Union
January 25, 1984

Our most precious resources, our greatest hope for the future, are the minds and hearts of our people, especially our children. We can help them build tomorrow by strengthening our community of shared values. This must be our third great goal. For us, faith, work, family, neighborhood, freedom, and peace are not just words; they're expressions of what America means, definitions of what makes us a good and loving people.

Families stand at the center of our society. And every family has a personal stake in promoting excellence in education. Excellence does not begin in Washington. A 600-percent increase in federal spending on education between 1960 and 1980 was accompanied by a steady decline in Scholastic Aptitude Test scores. Excellence must begin in our homes and neighborhood schools, where it's the responsibility of every parent and teacher and the right of every child.

During our first three years, we have joined bipartisan efforts to restore protection of the law to unborn children.

Now, I know this issue is very controversial. But unless and until it can be proven that an unborn child is not a living human being, can we justify assuming without proof that it isn't? No one has yet offered such proof; indeed, all the evidence is to the contrary. We should rise above bitterness and reproach, and if Americans could come together in a spirit of understanding and helping, then we could find positive solutions to the tragedy of abortion.

Economic recovery, better education, rededication to values all show the spirit of renewal gaining the upper hand. And all will improve family life in the eighties. But families need more. They need assurance that they and their loved ones can walk the streets of America without being afraid. Parents need to know their children will not be victims of child pornography and abduction. This year we will intensify our drive against these and other horrible crimes like sexual abuse and family violence.

National Religious Broadcasters Convention
January 30, 1984

Let's begin at the beginning. God is the center of our lives; the human family stands at the center of society; and our greatest hope for the future is in the faces of our children. Seven thousand Poles recently came to the christening of Maria Victoria Walesa, daughter of Danuat and Lech Walesa, to express their belief that solidarity of the family remains the foundation of freedom.

God's most blessed gift to his family is the gift of life. He sent us the Prince of Peace as a babe in a manger. I've said that we must be cautious in claiming God is on our side. I think the real question we must answer is, are we on his side?

I know what I'm about to say now is controversial, but I have to say it. This nation cannot continue turning a blind eye and a deaf ear to the taking of some 4,000 unborn cildren's lives every day. That's one every twenty-one seconds. One every twenty-one seconds.

We cannot pretend that America is preserving her first and highest ideal, the belief that each life is sacred, when we've permitted the deaths of 15 million helpless innocents since the Roe v. Wade decision—15 million children who will never laugh, never sing, never know the joy of human love, will never strive to heal the sick, feed the poor, or make peace among nations. Abortion has denied them the first and most basic of human rights. We are all infinitely poorer for their loss.

There's another grim truth we should face up to: Medical science doctors confirm that when the lives of the unborn are snuffed out, they often feel pain, pain that is long and agonizing.

This nation fought a terrible war so that black Americans would be guaranteed their God-given rights. Abraham Lincoln recognized that we could not survive as a free land when some could decide whether others should be free or slaves. Well, today another question begs to be asked: How can we survive as a free nation when some decide that others are not fit to live and should be done away with?

I believe no challenge is more important to the character of America than restoring the right to life to all human beings. Without that right, no other rights have meaning. "Suffer the little children to come unto me, and forbid them not, for such is the kingdom of God."

I will continue to support every effort to restore that protection, including the Hyde-Jepsen Respect Life Bill. I've asked for your all-out commitment, for the mighty power of your prayers, so that together we can convince our fellow countrymen that America should, can, and will preserve God's greatest gift.

Let us encourage those among us who are trying to provide positive alternatives to abortion—groups like Mom's House, House of His Creation in Pennsylvania, Jim McKee's Sav-A-Life in Texas, which I mentioned to you last year. Begun as a response to the call of a conscience, Sav-A-Life has become a crisis counseling center and saved twenty-two children since it was founded in 1981.

I think we're making progress in upholding the sanctity of life of infants born with physical or mental handicaps. The Department of Health and Human Services has now published final regulations to address cases such as Baby Doe in Bloomington. That child was denied lifesaving surgery and starved to death because he had Down's Syndrome and some people didn't think his life would be worth living.

Not too long ago I was privileged to meet in the Oval Office a charming little girl—filled with the joy of living. She was on crutches, but she swims, she rides horseback, and her smile steals your heart. She was born with the same defects as those Baby Does who have been denied the right to life. To see her, to see the love on the faces of her parents and their joy in her was the answer to this particular question.

Secretary Heckler and Surgeon General Koop deserve credit for designing regulations providing basic protections to the least among us. And the American Academy of Pediatrics and the National Association of Children's Hospitals have now affirmed a person's mental or physical handicap must not be the basis for deciding to withhold medical treatment.

Let me assure you of something else: We want parents to know their children will not be victims of child pornography. I look forward to signing a new bill now awaiting final action in a conference committee that will tighten our laws against child pornography. And we're concerned about enforcement of all the federal anti-obscenity laws.

Over the past year, the United States Customs Service

has increased by 200 percent its confiscation of obscene materials coming in across our borders. We're also intensifying our drive against crimes of family violence and sexual abuse. I happen to believe that protecting victims is just as important as safeguardng the rights of defendants.

Restoring the right to life and protecting people from violence and exploitation are important responsibilities. But as members of God's family we share another, and that is helping to build a foundation of faith and knowledge to prepare our children for the challenges of life. "Train up a child in the way he should go," Solomon wrote, "and when he is old he will not depart from it."

If we're to meet the challenge of educating for the space age, of opening eyes and minds to treasures of literature, music, and poetry, and of teaching values of faith, courage, responsibility, kindness and love, then we must meet these challenges as one people. And parents must take the lead. And I believe they are.

Conservative Political Action Conference
March 2, 1984

Not long ago I received a letter from a young woman named Kim. She was born with a birth defect, Spina Bifida, and given little chance to live. But her parents were willing to try a difficult and risky operation on her spine. It worked. And Kim wrote me: "I am now twenty-four years old. I do have some medical problems due to my birth defect. I have a lot of problems with my legs. But I'm walking. I can talk. I went to grade and high school, plus one year of college. I thank God every day for my parents and my life." And Kim said, "I wouldn't change it if I could."

Life was her greatest opportunity, and she made the

most of it. An opportunity society for all, reaching for its future with confidence, sustained by faith, fair play, and a conviction that good and courageous people flourish when they're free—this is the noble vision we share, a vision of a strong and prosperous America, at peace with itself and the world. Just as America has always been synonymous with freedom, so, too, should we become the symbol of peace across the Earth. I'm confident we can keep faith with that mission.

National Association of Evangelicals Convention
March 6, 1984

We must do our duty to generations not yet born. We cannot proclaim the noble ideal that human life is sacred, then turn our backs on the taking of some 4,000 unborn children's lives everyday. Abortion as a means of birth control must stop.

Many who seek abortions do so in harrowing circumstances. Often, they suffer deep personal trauma. Just as tolerance means accepting that many in good faith hold views different from our own, it also means that no man or woman should sit in judgment on another. If we could rise above bitterness and reproach, if Americans could come together in a spirit of understanding and helping, then we could find positive solutions to the tragedy of abortion—this we must do.

Visit to the Jeanne Jugan Residence
May 13, 1984

Since the Little Sisters of the Poor was founded in 1839, the order has spread to thirty-four countries on five continents and cared for more than a million of the elderly today, of my generation. And here in Washington, although this one is only a year old, it replaced one that was operated by the Little Sisters of the Poor for more than a century.

And throughout all these decades, you've cared for the elderly in our Capital . . . who had nowhere else to go. You've brought them into a warm and happy home. And you've given them, in addition to the necessities, the thing that only the love of others can bestow: Dignity.

I know that for your financial support, you depend on individual donations, and I can't think of any worthier cause than the Little Sisters of the Poor. And on behalf of all those you've done so very much to help, I thank you.

You know, Nancy and I, coming down here from Camp David on the helicopter, couldn't help but be thinking about this particular day and what it was. I think about my mother. Nelle was a little woman, auburn hair, and, I realize now, had a strength through some very trying times that held our family together. We were poor, but the government didn't come around and tell us we were, so we didn't know it. And probably we didn't know it because Nelle was always finding someone that was worse off than we were that needed help.

And my father was hard-working. He had a sense of humor. He also had a very great problem, but my mother saw that my brother and I, from the time we were children, understood that problem and that it was something—a sickness, and that he was not to be blamed, but to be loved.

And she taught us about life, I think, by her deeds as well as her works. She had never gone beyond—in education—beyond elementary school, but she had a different kind of education that I think has been imprinted and a faith that I know now has been bestowed on me.

I'd like to just tell a little anecdote about it. Some

years after I was in Hollywood, I was able to bring my parents out there, and she immediately started finding people. And one she found was a county tubercular sanitarium that could provide, as a public institution could of that kind, the necessary care, but certainly failed in some of the home-like atmosphere that was necessary.

And my mother went to work, and she visited that place regularly. She arranged for movies to be shown and for television and things of that kind that they had never had before. And one night—and she has left us now—but one night I was at a banquet. I was the speaker at a banquet. And a few years ago, banquet food wasn't of the same quality that it is today. And the waiter that was coming along leaned down to me and whispered and said, "Would you rather have a big steak than what we're serving here?"

"Well," I said, "if that's possible, yes," because I did a lot of banquet speaking in those days, and I'd had enough of banquet food. Well, he arrived back with the nicest, big T-bone steak you ever saw and put it in front of me.

Now, in the meantime, I had decided that he had to be a motion picture fan, and he must have liked my pictures. And I was basking in that kind of reflected glory. And as he put the steak down, he leaned down and whispered in my ear, "Anytime, for a relative of Nelle Reagan's. I used to be a patient at Olive View Sanitarium."

But Nancy, at the same time—and this is a coincidence; thank heaven, Nancy's mother is still with us—Nancy's mother, living in Chicago, was one of a kind also. I don't think there was a policeman or a doorman or a cabdriver or anyone like that in Chicago that didn't know Edith Davis, because she, too, was always engaged in good works. And we saw a classic example of that.

Nancy and I got off the train, the New York Twentieth Century Limited in Chicago, in the midst of a blizzard and laden with bags and baggage and so forth from the trip we'd been on. Not a redcap, not a porter in sight and everyone struggling with their bags and everything. And we—this whole length of the train to go— all of a sudden looked down, and here came Nancy's mother, arm in arm with two redcaps.

And as she got closer, we could hear, she was asking the one about his children. She knew his children's names, knew all about them, what grade they were in. . . . [She asked the] other one about his wife's operation. She knew all about that, too. And [she] just happened to stop by us and say, "Oh, these are my children. Could you give them a hand with their bags?" And a whole trainload of people saw us stride down the platform with Nancy's mother and with the two porters, and they were still trying to manage with their bags, and we had plenty of help.

But I think things like this make me understand what Abe Lincoln was feeling when he said, "All that I am or hope to be, I owe to my mother."

And I know there are many of you mothers in this room. I also know that here are others who live as mothers live, the Little Sisters of the Poor, seventeen who are residents in this home and together with the 4,500 Little Sisters around the world who have chosen to give of themselves completely in humble service to their fellow men and women. The residents are your family. Your prayers and hard work have made this a very friendly and, it's very obvious, a joyful home.

And thank you all for allowing us to share this special day with you. And we wish each one of you a very happy and rewarding Mother's Day and the blessings of our beloved God.

EIGHT

ONE NATION UNDER GOD

The President's Statements on America's Spiritual Heritage

Blessed is the nation whose God is the Lord (Psalm 33:12a, TLB).

National Prayer Breakfast
February 4, 1982

I also believe this blessed land was set apart in a very special way, a country created by men and women who came here not in search of gold, but in search of God. They would be free people, living under the law with faith in their Maker and their future.

Sometimes it seems we've strayed from that noble beginning, from our conviction that standards of right and wrong do exist and must be lived up to. God, the source of our knowledge, has been expelled from the classroom. He gives us his greatest blessing—life—and yet many would condone the taking of innocent life. We expect him to protect us in a crisis, but turn away from him too often in our day-to-day living. I wonder if he isn't waiting for us to wake up.

National Religious Broadcasters Convention
February 9, 1982

I've always believed that we were put here for a reason, that there is a path somehow, a divine plan for all of us and for each one of us. And I've also always believed that America was set apart in a special way, that it was put here between the oceans to be found by a certain kind of people, based on a quality that these people had in that they came from every corner of the world. And a country then was created by men and women who came not for gold but mainly in search of God. They would be free people, living under the law, with faith in their Maker and in their future.

It's been written that the most sublime figure in American history was George Washington on his knees in the snow at Valley Forge. He personified a people who knew that it was not enough to depend on their own courage and goodness, that they must also seek help from God— their Father and Preserver.

Where did we begin to lose sight of that noble beginning, of our conviction that standards of right and wrong do exist and must be lived up to? Do we really think that we can have it both ways, that God will protect us in a time of crisis even as we turn away from him in our day-to-day life?

It's time to realize, I think, that we need God more than he needs us. But millions of Americans haven't forgotten. They know we've been on a toboggan slide, and they're determined to do something about it. And I'm honored to stand before you, thirty-five hundred of their most effective and courageous leaders. And let me say, I do not agree with those who accuse you of trying to impose your views on others. If we have come to the point in America where any attempt to see traditional values reflected in public policy would leave one open to irresponsible charges, then I say the entire structure of our free society is threatened. The first amendment was not written to protect the people from religious values; it was written to protect those values from government tyranny.

Alabama State Legislature
March 15, 1982

To those who cite the First Amendment as reason for excluding God from more and more of our institutions and everyday life, may I just say: The First Amendment of the Constitution was not written to protect the people of this country from religious values; it was written to protect religious values from government tyranny.

National Day of Prayer
May 6, 1982

How can we hope to retain our freedom through the generations if we fail to teach our young that our liberty springs from an abiding faith in our Creator?

Thomas Jefferson once said, "Almighty God created the mind free." But current interpretation of our Constitution holds that the minds of our children cannot be free to pray to God in public schools. No one will ever convince me that a moment of voluntary prayer will harm a child or threaten a school or state. But I think it can strengthen our faith in a Creator who alone has the power to bless America.

Ceremony in Observance of National Day of Prayer
May 6, 1982

Together, let us take up the challenge to reawaken America's religious and moral heart, recognizing that a deep and abiding faith in God is the rock upon which this great nation was founded.

U.S. League of Savings Associations
November 16, 1982

Above all, let us remember the mountain of strength that offers the greatest hope and inspiration for all. I believe with all my heart that standing up for America means standing up for the God who has so blessed our land. We need God's help to guide our nation through stormy seas. But we can't expect him to protect America in a crisis if we just leave him over on the shelf in our day-to-day living. There's a lovely old hymn which says: "When morning lights the eastern skies, O Lord Thy mercy show, on Thee alone our hope relies, let us Thy kindness know."

National Religious Broadcasters Convention
January 31, 1983

I've always believed that this blessed land was set apart in a special way, that some divine plan placed this great continent here between the two oceans to be found by people from every corner of the earth—people who had a special love for freedom and the courage to uproot themselves, leave their homeland and friends, to come to a strange land. And, when coming here, they created something new in all the history of mankind—a country where man is not beholden to government; government is beholden to man.

Meeting with Jewish Leaders
February 2, 1983

America knows God's blessings. Our cup truly runneth over. We seek only to share the blessings of liberty, peace, and prosperity.

Conservative Political Action Conference
February 18, 1983

Our founding fathers prohibited a federal establishment of religion, but there is no evidence that they intended to set up a wall of separation between the state and religious belief itself.

The evidence of this is all around us. In the Declaration of Independence alone there are no fewer than four mentions of a Supreme Being. "In God We Trust" is engraved on our coinage. The Supreme Court opens its proceedings with a religious invocation. And the Congress opens each day with prayer from its chaplains.

National Association of Evangelicals Convention
March 8, 1983

Freedom prospers when religion is vibrant and the rule of law under God is acknowledged. When our founding fathers passed the First Amendment, they sought to protect churches from government interference. They never intended to construct a wall of hostility between government and the concept of religious belief itself.

The evidence of this permeates our history and our government. The Declaration of Independence mentions the Supreme Being no less than four times. "In God We Trust" is engraved on our coinage. The Supreme Court opens its proceedings with a religious invocation. And the members of Congress open their sessions with a prayer. I just happen to believe that the school children of the United States are entitled to the same privileges as Supreme Court Justices and Congressmen.

Dinner Honoring Senator Jesse Helms of North Carolina
June 16, 1983

We Americans are blessed in so many ways. We're a nation under God, a living and loving God. But Thomas Jefferson warned us, "I tremble for my country when I reflect that God is just." We cannot expect him to protect us in a crisis if we turn away from him in our everyday living. But you know, he told us what to do in II Chronicles. Let us reach out to him. He said, "If my people, which are called by my name, shall humble themselves and pray and seek my face and turn from their wicked ways, then will I hear from heaven and will forgive their sin and will heal their land."
Captive Nations Week
July 19, 1983
The Prophet Isaiah admonished the world, "Bind up the brokenhearted to proclaim liberty to the captives." Some twenty-five centuries later, philosophers would declare that "the cause of freedom is the cause of God."

American Bar Association Meeting
August 1, 1983

It's not good enough to have equal access to our law; we must also have equal access to the higher law—the law of God. George Washington warned that morality could not prevail in exclusion of religious principles. And Jefferson asked, "Can the liberties of a nation be thought secure, when we've removed their only firm basis, a conviction in the minds of people that these liberties are the gifts of God?"

We must preserve the noble promise of the American dream for every man, woman, and child in this land. And make no mistake, we can preserve it, and we will. That promise was not created by America. It was given to America as a gift from a loving God—a gift proudly recognized by the language of liberty in the world's greatest charters of freedom: our Declaration of Independence, the Constitution, and the Bill of Rights.

Seventy-seven years after the Constitution was adopted, Lord Acton said of the men who had written it that "they had solved with astonishing and unexampled success two problems which had hitherto baffled the capacity of the most enlightened nations: they had contrived a system of Federal Government which . . . increased the National power, and yet respected local liberties and authorities; they had founded it on the principle of equality, without surrendering the securities for property and freedom." Well, here, for the first time in the history of the world, was a system in which man would not be beholden to government; government would be beholden to man.

The explicit promise in the Declaration that we're endowed by our Creator with certain inalienable rights was meant for all of us. It wasn't meant to be limited or perverted by special privilege or by double standards that favor one group over another. It is a principle for eternity, America's deepest treasure. Father Hesburgh reminded us, our rights are "corollaries of the great proposition, at the heart of Western civilization, that every . . . person is a *ressacra,* a sacred reality, and as such is entitled to the opportunity of fulfilling those great human potentials with which God has endowed man."

The promise of America, the character of our people, the thrust of our history, and the challenge of our future all point toward a higher mission: to build together a society of opportunity, a society that rewards excellence, bound by a body of laws nourished with the spirit of faith, equity, responsibility, and compassion. The streets of America would not be paved with gold; they would be paved with opportunity. Success would depend upon personal initiative and merit.

Thomas Jefferson said his criteria for honor and status was not wealth, but virtue and talent. In "Abraham Lincoln: The Prairie Years," Carl Sandburg wrote that Lincoln believed "the accent and stress was to be on opportunity, on equal chance, equal access to the resources of life, liberty, and the pursuit of happiness. To give man this equal chance in life was the aim, the hope, the flair of glory, spoken by the Declaration of Independence."

Trusting in God and helping one another, we can and will preserve the dream of America, the last best hope of man on earth.

Christian Religious Organizations
October 13, 1983

The founding fathers believed that faith in God was the key to our being a good people and America's becoming a great nation. George Washington kissed the Bible at his inauguration. And to those who would have government separate us from religion, he had these words: "Reason and experience both forbid us to expect that national morality can prevail in exclusion of religious principle." And Ben Franklin, at the time when they were struggling with what was to be the American Constitution, finally one day said to those who were working with him, that "without God's help, we shall succeed in this political building no better than the builders of Babel." And if we ever forget that, we're lost. From that day on they opened all of the constitutional meetings with prayer.

Government is not supposed to wage war against God and religion, not in the United States of America.

State of the Union Address
January 25, 1984

Carl Sandburg said, "I see America not in the setting sun of a black night of despair. . . . I see America in the crimson light of a rising sun fresh from the burning, creative hand of God. . . . I see great days ahead for men and women of will and vision."

I've never felt more strongly that America's best days and democracy's best days lie ahead. We're a powerful force for good. With faith and courage, we can perform great deeds and take freedom's next step. And we will. We will carry on the tradition of a good and worthy people who have brought light where there was darkness, warmth where there was cold, medicine where there was disease, food where there was hunger, and peace where there was only bloodshed.

Let us be sure that those who come after will say of us in our time, that in our time we did everything that could be done. We finished the race; we kept them free; we kept the faith.

A Salute to Free Enterprise
January 26, 1984

We are a nation under God. I've always believed that this blessed land was set apart in a special way, that some divine plan placed this great continent here between the oceans to be found by people from every corner of the earth who had a special love for freedom and the courage to uproot themselves, leave homeland and friends, to come to a strange land. And coming here they created something new in all the history of mankind—a land where man is not beholden to government; government is beholden to man.

George Washington believed that religion, morality, and brotherhood were the pillars of society. He said you couldn't have morality without religion. And yet today we're told that to protect the First Amendment we must expel God, the source of all knowledge, from our children's classrooms. Well, pardon me, but the First Amendment was not written to protect the American people from religion; the first amendment was written to protect the American people from government tyranny.

Indeed, there is nothing in the Constitution at all about public education and prayer. There is, however, something very pertinent in the act that gave birth to our public school system—a national act, if you will. It called for public education to see that our children—and quoting from that act—"learned about religion and morality."

Well, the time has come for Congress to give a majority of American families what they want for their children—a constitutional amendment making it unequivocally clear that children can hold voluntary prayer in their schools.

We can make America stronger not just economically and militarily, but also morally and spiritually. We can make our beloved country the source of all the dreams and opportunities she was placed on this good earth to provide. We

need only to believe in each other and in the God who
has so blessed our land.

Conservative Political Action Conference
March 2, 1984

In *Year of Decision, 1846,* Bernard DeVoto explained what
drove our ancestors to conquer the West, create a nation,
and open up a continent. If you take away the dream, you
take away the power of the spirit. If you take away the
belief in a greater future, you cannot explain America—
that we're a people who believed there was a promised land;
we were a people who believed we were chosen by God
to create a greater world.

NINE

IN BOTH WORD AND DEED

There exists in America today a state of moral confusion, and it touches every area of society. All it really takes to be convinced of this is a quick perusal of any newsstand in the nation. Newspapers and magazines are an accurate reflection of the values that are in vogue.

Moral confusion operates nationally the same way it operates in an individual's life. Usually the "confused" person is struggling with right versus wrong. The so-called confusion exists while the individual is trying to justify the wrong action.

It is interesting to note that the Bible never applies the word *confusion* to this type of behavior. Rather, Scripture speaks of it as rebellion—a turning away from God's moral absolutes.

At this point, words and their definitions become vitally important. When people, or nations, try to justify wrong actions they begin by modifying the language, by playing semantic games, by verbally diminishing the moral seriousness of their rebellion.

Charles Krauthammer in a July 9, 1984, *Time* essay makes this observation: "Perhaps the deepest cause of moral confusion is the state of language itself, language that has been bleached of its moral distinctions, turned neutral, value-free, 'nonjudgmental.' When that happens, moral discourse becomes difficult, moral distinctions impossible, and moral debate incomprehensible. If abortion is simply 'termination of pregnancy,' the moral equivalent of, say, removing a tumor, how to account for a movement of serious people dedicated to its abolition? If homosexuality is merely 'sexual preference'—if a lover's sex is as much a matter of taste as, say, hair color . . . then why the to-do over two men dancing at Disneyland? But there is a fuss because there is a difference. One can understand neither with language that refuses to make distinctions."

While it is more accurate spiritually to say this language problem is a symptom of rebellion rather than a cause, the point remains the same. Words are important. Proverbs says: "The tongue has the power of life and death."

There is a moral rebellion under way in our nation today. There is war between those who uphold Judeo-Christian values as the standard for our society and those who favor a value-free system. And there are many battles of words being waged on several fronts.

Proverbs 28:2a says: "When a country is rebellious [*read 'confused'*], it has many leaders." In other words, there are many generals leading these battles of words in this moral war. In modern terminology they are called *spokespersons.* Confusion reigns. However, the second part of this verse offers hope: "But a man of understanding and knowledge maintains order."

It is God's intention and purpose for those he raises up in positions of national leadership to maintain order. Romans 13:1–6 contains the best single description of God's view of civil authority. "Everyone must submit himself to the governing authorities, for there is no authority except that which God has established. The authorities that exist have been established by God.

"Consequently, he who rebels against the authority is rebelling against what God has instituted, and those who do so will bring judgment on themselves. For rulers hold no terror for those who do fight, but for those who do wrong. Do you want to be free from fear of the one in authority? Then do what is right and he will commend you. . . . But if you do wrong, be afraid, for he does not bear the sword for nothing. He is God's servant, an agent of wrath to bring punishment on the wrongdoer. Therefore, it is necessary to submit to the authorities, not only because of possible punishment but also because of conscience.

"This is also why you pay taxes, for the authorities are God's servants, who give their full time to governing."

The key phrase in this section of Scripture is "the authorities are God's servants." Every leader of every nation is God's servant. God takes a keen interest in who is appointed or elected to govern each nation, and he works through these leaders to accomplish his purposes on earth.

It is interesting to note that these rulers, kings, and presidents are God's servants by his choice—not their choice. This is why it is significant when a leader of a nation chooses God. Not only does God have him, but he also has God.

When a national leader has a relationship with the God of the universe, spiritual blessings and gifts are released to the people of that nation. These blessings and gifts take many forms and affect all aspects of a nation's life. The Bible specifically speaks of virtues such as stability (Proverbs 29:4), order (Proverbs 28:2), and just laws (Proverbs 8:15) and says they are direct results of godly leadership.

Two other very important national blessings that are released through righteous leadership are that of hope and freedom. These virtues are stressed three times within two chapters of the Book of Proverbs. Proverbs 28:12, 28 and 29:2 say that when the righteous triumph, there is great elation; but when the wicked rise to power, the people groan and go into hiding. In other words, godly leadership creates a liberty in society that allows confidence, hope, and private enterprise to flourish. This naturally affects everything from the economy to personal freedom.

It is clear from looking at Ronald Reagan's life and his presidential statements that he is a godly leader, a man of spiritual understanding and knowledge. As president he has maintained order by providing moral leadership for a nation in moral rebellion.

His message to America has remained simple yet powerful, consistent yet always challenging—"We are one nation under God." Regardless of the audience or the topic, this theme has served as the foundation for his remarks. Often he has delivered this message at great political risk. But like them or not, no one can say his words have lacked a moral emphasis.

"America needs God more than God needs America. If we ever forget that we are one nation under God, then we will become just one nation under."

There is hardly any room for misunderstanding in these words or the meaning behind them. In just this way, President Reagan has issued a clear sound in calling the nation to turn to God. First Corinthians 14:8 says: "If the trumpet does not sound a clear call, who will get ready for battle?" Those following the president's lead have heard the trumpets sound.

Not only has Ronald Reagan provided national moral leadership, the president has also created a climate in which moral deeds can flourish. He has not simply talked about his vision for America, he has made it practical, which has encouraged others to do the same. Ronald Reagan's faith is not without works.

Three themes that have been especially strong throughout the course of the Reagan presidency have been strengthening the economy, rebuilding the nation's defense capability, and supporting traditional family values. Polls indicate that many in our nation have experienced the optimism and freedom that has come with President Reagan's leadership in each of these areas. He gets high marks overall for the way he has handled his job, and much of the nation feels he is on the right track.

The president's faith in action can perhaps be best illustrated by considering a variety of his social and economic policy initiatives that have directly affected the family.

One of the major tenants of the president's economic policy has been to bring relief to the family unit. As a result of the president's economic plan, inflation has dropped, taxes have been cut, and interest rates have decreased. To the average family in 1983 this meant that a typical income of $29,300 was worth $2,500 more than if inflation had still been at the 1980 rate. In addition, consider the following:

—The average family also paid some $700 less in federal income tax for 1983 than if 1980 tax rates had been in place.

—Statistics show that lower interest rates have put home ownership in reach for approximately 11 million families who could not afford a home when the president took office.

—The so-called marriage penalty has been greatly reduced—saving two-earner couples about $300 per year when each makes about $15,000.

—The tax credit for child care has been raised from $400 for one child of a working mother to a maximum of $720 per family.

—Toughened child support enforcement produced $170 million in 1982 alone from fathers who abandoned welfare families.

—Rules governing individual retirement accounts (IRA's) have been liberalized to allow larger contributions by women who work outside the home and also for home-makers with no earned income.

—Spending in the fiscal 1984 budget for ten key programs for needy children is up 25 percent from 1980 levels.

—School lunches are being provided free to about 10 million low-income students, an increase over previous programs.

Other family-related issues that have received the president's attention and more extensive media coverage are abortion, the handicapped newborn, drug abuse, human rights, tuition tax credits, and school prayer. In each area, the president has initiated action favorable to the family.

While the debate will go on about President Reagan's policies, no one can ever say that he never acted on what he believed to be right. As long as he is President of the United States, the traditional moral values taught in the Bible will be brought to bear on all the issues his administration seeks to affect.

As usual he says it best: "May we have faith in our God and all the good we can do with his help. May we stand firm in the hope of making America all that she can be—a nation of opportunity and prosperity and a force for peace and good will among nations. And may we remain steadfast in our love for this green and gentle land and the freedom that she offers."